IDENTITY RESET

A Guide to
Getting Out of Your Boxes

Karen Tyler

Karen D. Tyler, M.S.W
Certified Professional Co-Active Life Coach

Softcover ISBN: 979-8-9890630-0-0

E-book ISBN: 979-8-9890630-1-7

Printed in the United States of America

Cover Photo and Interior Design: Diamond Joy Castine'

Requests for information and for bulk orders should be addressed to:

KDT Global Consulting

www.kdtglobalconsulting.com

ktyler@kdtglobalconsulting.com

 PUBLISHED BY: Upward Forward Onward Press, DISCLAIMER AND/OR LEGAL NOTICES, while all attempts have been made to verify information provided in this book and its ancillary materials, neither the author nor publisher assumes any responsibility for errors, inaccuracies or omissions and is not responsible for any financial loss by customer in any manner. Any slights of people or organizations are unintentional. If advice concerning legal, financial, accounting or related matters is needed, the services of a qualified professional should be sought. This book and its associated ancillary materials, including verbal and written training, are not intended for use as a source of legal, financial or accounting advice. This book is written and shares my journey and my experience of how things have impacted and shaped my life. I don't speak on behalf of others, my family, families, races, cultures, genders or religions. The information stated and shared is not a generalization nor a representative of the majority or minority. The content does not represent providing services, nor solutions, physically, emotionally, or mentally. Any support needed in these areas including mental health services/support are to be addressed by your professional service provider. EARNINGS & INCOME DISCLAIMER With respect to the reliability, accuracy, timeliness, usefulness, adequacy, completeness, and/ or suitability of information provided in this book, Karen D. Tyler, KDT Global Consulting, Reset Rethink Solutions, its partners, associates, affiliates, consultants, and/or presenters make no warranties, guarantees, representations, or claims of any kind. Readers' results will vary depending on several factors. All claims or representations as to income earnings are not to be considered as average earnings. Testimonials are not representative. This book and all products and services are for educational and informational purposes only. Use caution and see the advice of qualified professionals. Check with your accountant, attorney or professional advisor before acting on this or any information. You agree that Karen D. Tyler and/or Karen D. Tyler, KDT Global Consulting, Reset Rethink Solutions, or any affiliate of, is not responsible for the choices, success or failure of your personal, business, health or financial decisions relating to any information presented by Karen Tyler, KDT Global Consulting, Reset Rethink Solutions, or company products/services. Earnings potential is entirely dependent on the efforts, skills and application of the individual person. Any examples, stories, references, or case studies are for illustrative purposes only and should not be interpreted as testimonies and/or examples of what reader and/or consumers can generally expect from the information. No representation of any part of this information, materials and/or seminar training are guarantees or promises for actual performance. Any statements, strategies, concepts, techniques, exercises and ideas in the information, materials and/or seminar training offered are simply opinion or experience, and thus should not be misinterpreted as promises, typical results or guarantees (expressed or implied). The author, Karen D. Tyler, and publisher, Upward Forward Onward Press, or any of Karen D. Tyler's businesses, affiliates or any representatives shall in no way, under any circumstances, be held liable to any party (or third party) for any direct, indirect, punitive, special, incidental or other consequential damages arising directly or indirectly from any use of books, materials and or seminar trainings, which is provided "as is," and without warranties.

WHAT OTHERS ARE SAYING ABOUT KAREN TYLER AND KAREN'S STRATEGIES

"Karen utilizes a strategic approach to identify specifically how to serve others. She subscribes to the idea that people are experts in identifying their own needs."
Roscoe Sullivan, Las Vegas, Nevada

"Working with Karen you can expect compassion and transformation. Her coaching strategies guide her clients to find their authentic voice, and a path forward to living a life of purpose."
Pam Panser, Toronto, Canda

"When Karen is faced with adversity, she leans into it, she survives and comes out on the other side. She then applies the lessons she learned to her life. I have no doubt that this is how she found her voice. Karen is equipped to help others grow and find their voice."
Karen Cauthorne, Fredericksburg, VA

"Karen Tyler has an extraordinary approach to teaching and coaching that easily boosts one's confidence and shines a spotlight on their intelligence. I have vastly improved my ability to problem solve because of her expertise and guidance."
Samantha Charles, Las Vegas, Nevada

"Get ready for an exciting new period of growth and prosperity with Karen's strategies. If you know you want to do something that changes the world, then Karen has a method to help you unlock potential and live a life of purpose."
Chaplain Elsa Elise Black, MBA, Author of Battered but Not Broken, Cincinnati, Ohio

"Whether you're attending one of Karen's training events, or engaging in a conversation with her, you'll be inspired, and challenged to be the highest version of yourself." Wanda Porter, Las Vegas, NV

Retail Investment: $14.99
Special Quantity Available Upon Request

To Place an Order Contact:
KDT Global Consulting
www.kdtglobalconsulting.com
info@kdtglobalconsulting.com

THE IDEAL PROFESSIONAL SPEAKER
FOR YOUR NEXT EVENT!

Any organization that wants to develop their people to become "extraordinary," needs to hire, KAREN D. TYLER for a keynote and/or workshop training!

TO CONTACT KAREN D. TYLER:
KDT Global Consulting
www.kdtglobalconsulting.com
info@kdtglobalconsulting.com

THE IDEAL COACH FOR YOU!

If you're ready to overcome challenges, have major breakthroughs and achieve higher levels, then you will love having KAREN D. TYLER as your coach!

If you or your organization is ready to develop, expand and/or grow while shifting old patterns and strategies, while getting out of your identified box(es), that are not profitable; then partnering with KAREN D. TYLER as your individual life coach, or your organizational coach, is the next step for you to take.

TO CONTACT KAREN TYLER:
KDT Global Consulting
www.kdtglobalconsulting.com
info@kdtglobalconsulting.com

DEDICATION

It is with respect, admiration and sincere appreciation that I dedicate this book to you, each person reading this book. This book is also dedicated to my loving family. My heart's desire is for you to live YOUR life. Hit the reset button, get out of the box, and be who you really are as you live a life of freedom.

TABLE OF CONTENTS

Read This:

A Message to You:
GET READY, GET SET, GO!!

Get Ready! Get Set! Go!

Let's Go!

How long will you continue to conform, to "go along" just to fit in? Consider the historical and generational patterns, traditions, or expectations from others that constrain you. They constrain you much like a tightly woven wicker basket or leave you tangled like an enormous ball of yarn.

Imagine this, at the end of each day, you exhale a deep breath of relief, alone in your own space. You reflect on life and your daily experiences, replaying them repeatedly. On one hand, you feel an internal despair, yearning for someone to unravel your complexities, one knot at a time. On the other, there's a sense of relief in these moments, where you can be your authentic self and simply "be me."

Do you wake up and show up, time after time, sensing something is missing? As days, months, and years pass, do you feel that you're not leading a fulfilling life?

First, prepare to embark on your personal journey of self-discovery, as you ask yourself a profound question, "Who am I?" The good news is that you have the chance to explore and find out who you truly are. What an incredible privilege and opportunity! The aim of this book is not only to help you understand and discover your identity but also to share my own journey and experiences of self-discovery. We all have the extraordinary opportunity to delve into our true selves.

Remember, you're not alone in asking, "Who am I?" In my role as a teacher, speaker, and empowerment life coach, I assist others in contemplating this very question as they search for and explore their own answers. "How did I get here?" When will it be my time?

These are all great questions and the first steps during your self-discovery journey in pursuit of discovering your identity. Give yourself a pat on your back for taking one step forward.

Get ready to be you. To be authentic and honest with yourself. Not being yourself, not being authentic and honest to yourself, will land you in a place of living an unfulfilled life. You will struggle to survive in life instead of thriving. Instead, let's live a life of freedom as you live YOUR life, as opposed to attempting to measure up to the historical and generational patterns, traditions, and expectations of others, and not succumb to living by "we don't do it that way," "this is the way it's always been," or "that's just the way we do it." Wow!

What does a shift of mindset from being shaped by the box of race, family, roles, and religion, or your self-identified box/es, look like?

Go on a journey with me as we discuss four areas of the self-identity journey. First, we'll explore understanding your identity as you dive into exploring the question, "Who am I?" This is important because what you think, feel, do, and say impacts you and others as you pass on information and behaviors from one generation to the next (intentionally and unintentionally).

Secondly, you will learn how to use what I term the two-step emotional CPR.ed process (stay tuned; we'll discuss this in a minute). This process will assist you in viewing situations from different perspectives. It will also guide you to look at both sides of the coin as you experience life and situations that present themselves.

Thirdly, you will discover how being stuffed into boxes, being confined or defined by your boxes of race, family, roles, and religion, or your self-identified boxes, shapes and impacts your identity. Your upbringing, environment, and experiences influence your thinking, feeling, and behavior, both in this present moment, in the short-term and long-term future, and down the road for years to come.

The boxes just mentioned are not inclusive of all boxes that exist in life. There are other boxes (i.e., superiority, poverty, financial, fear, people pleasing, political affiliation, socio-economic status, grief, depression, oppression, occupation, etc.) that also exist. I invite you to identify the boxes that are present in your life.

Fourthly, you will understand and become attuned to how your limiting beliefs interfere with your thriving in life and experiencing a life of freedom.

My awakening moment validated my never-spoken internal thoughts and feelings and helped me realize that something was missing in my life. It is at that point I began to put the puzzle pieces together. You too can also begin to put the pieces of your puzzle together. The emotional CPR.ed process can be used as a springboard to thrust you forward. The process will also support you as you decide how to get out of your boxes or determine how to cohabitate in a healthy fashion, within your box of race, family, roles, and religion or within your self-identified boxes.

CPR.ed Process

Settle in, get comfortable, and get ready to be the true and authentic you as you apply the emotional CPR.ed process. The first part of the process supports you to gain Clarity, understand Purpose (or the why), followed by no longer living in denial as you stand face to face with Reality in your life.

The second part of the emotional CPR.ed process allows you to give yourself permission to feel each Emotion you experience. Keep in mind your emotions are real, and emotions for everyone are normal. So, pause and take your time as you experience and manage each of your emotions during the process. Doing so will support you to shift your mindset as you transition and make Decisions for “you”.

As you embark on this journey of exploration, you’ll connect with your core beliefs and speak your truth about various aspects of your identity, such as race, family, roles, and religion, or within any self-identified boxes. You have the power to decide how the historical and generational patterns, traditions, and expectations of others play out in your life. You get to determine what serves you now and what no longer serves you.

Remember, you are the captain of your life and bear the responsibility of managing it. What are your life values? Honoring and upholding historical and generational patterns, traditions, and expectations of others might look different for you, and that’s perfectly okay. Different is just different. The goal is to navigate your emotions wisely, making decisions that honor your true self.

You are not alone in this endeavor. I, too, found myself trying to figure out life, while also attempting to live out societal expectations and norms, that were often burdened by “supposed to” “need to,” “ought to,” and “should” that’s have imposed by others. This people-pleasing tendency left me dishonoring my own values and needs while satisfying other people, their opinion and their expectations.

What does this mean to you? It means you can live out what I learned. I learned, I don’t have to succumb to those expectations, and instead, honor and respect others while remaining authentic and honest with yourself. Setting boundaries and communicating your needs are essential as you articulate what works best for you.

I was stuck in several areas of my life and applying the emotional CPR.ed process helped me become unstuck. As I teach, speak to, and coach others, I witness people moving from being stuck to taking steps forward, experiencing “aha” moments, and embracing their realities.

Reflect on how your ‘boxes’ affect you. What does freedom from these constraints look like for you?

Understanding the Boxes

Although there are many other boxes (i.e., inferiority, anger, guilt, shame, anxiety, hurt, trust/mistrust, helplessness, hopelessness, or people-pleasing), we will only discuss four boxes. The boxes of race, family, roles, and religion may or may not apply to you. If they don't apply to you, I invite you to identify boxes that may be present in your life.

If they do apply to you, keep in mind, although you may relate to the boxes, your experience within them will be different. With this, as you read, pause and reflect on your experience. If the boxes don't apply to you, identify the boxes that are important in your life as you pause and reflect on your experience.

Race (or Culture) Box

This box interferes with and prohibits you from living your life to the fullest, from living your wildest dreams, and from living your best life. For some people I have journeyed with, their experience of constantly hearing statements like, "No, not you," "This is not for you," "You can't," or "You have to" sometimes made them feel numb or become desensitized, while "complying" to said expectations. For some of you, hearing statements like, "Yes you," "You are more than," "That does not apply to you," or "Those people…" may contradict your values.

Limiting messages may not support how you feel or what you believe, and as a result, contradicts with your life values. This causes confusion, hopelessness, tiredness, depletion, defeat, emptiness and forces you to wear a mask. But you don't have to remain there; instead, rise above the limiting messages and shift your mindset. No more people-pleasing!

Family Box

You might feel the urge to break free from the constraining historical and generational patterns, traditions, and expectations of others. You may feel suffocated by familial expectations, bombarded with messages like "You're just like…," "You will never be…," or "You have to…." You may also feel ignored, unseen, unloved, or unappreciated. Or you may feel inadequate, insignificant, or voiceless.

However, you don't have to feel that way, nor accept those messages as your truth. You are allowed to voice your own truth. As you stand in your truth and embrace reality, you no longer must accept dismissive messages such as "Because I said so" or "Do as I say, not as I do." You have the responsibility and the right to think for yourself, to reject conformity birthed from "group think," and not allow others to dictate your feelings, thoughts and behaviors, nor your actions, opinions, and decisions.

Roles/Gender Box

The box of roles, including gender, sibling position, and leadership roles, can be restrictive. These roles often lead to confusion reinforced by statements like "Girls or women should or shouldn't…" or "Boys and men should or shouldn't…" You don't have to conform to stereotypical expectations, like the idea that females should be emotional while males are expected to "suck it up," "don't cry," and "be strong."

Who decided these norms?

Striving to meet these expectations may leave you feeling overwhelmed, as if you are drowning in a bottomless sea of suppressed emotions, trying to fit into the roles dictated by others.

Religion Box

Let's examine the paralyzing box of religion. I've grappled with religious practices and legalism, as have many others. It's normal to experience internal conflict as you begin to discern your true beliefs and honor your values.

What do you genuinely believe about religion or belief practices? Not what you've been told, not the historical and generational patterns, traditions and expectations of others. Nor what you've been told about the rituals, routines, or the legalism of religion that you've accepted, adopted, accommodated, or adhere to. Not even what you believe about the oppressive messages like "You have to," "Do more," "Do the right thing," or "You can't," and "Don't…" These beliefs might conflict with your true beliefs or values.

So, my friend, what do you truly believe about your religion or belief system?

The box of religion, religious practices, legalism or belief systems, may leave you feeling angry, hurt, in pain, distrustful, or disappointed. As a result, you may build walls to protect yourself, your mind, and your peace. Being protective of yourself may indirectly position you to disconnect from others, from those who love you and care about, and from living your life within a community. This can hinder your progress in life, and in turn cause you to feel restricted and overwhelmed. Hence the need to dig within yourself as you explore the question, "Who am I?"

Who can relate to any of these boxes? If not, what boxes exist in your life? Take a moment and reflect. What do you truly believe, deep down inside?

Walking Your New Journey

Wow! The many boxes are confining, restricting, limiting, and heavy! Being in one, two, three, or all the identified boxes may leave you feeling like you are on a merry-go-round or on a roller coaster. Being in these boxes may be the underlying cause of deep-rooted emotions of anger, depression, anxiety, stress, medical conditions, or being overwhelmed as you spiral out of control. If this is you or someone you know, rest assured, there's hope, there is light at the end of the tunnel. What's needed to undo who you have become is right inside of you. Your identity, who you really are, is waiting patiently on you to embrace "you."

Today is a new day! No more being silent, not using your voice, and not having an opinion, because you've embraced someone else's opinion as your own. No more living up to the "said" expectations, living your life for someone else, living someone else's life, nor living life in someone's shadow.

What will you say, "no" to? As you say "no," what are you then saying "yes" to?

The rumbling in your soul is screaming for you to hit the reset button and dance out of your boxes. Get ready to fling the top off your box as you get out and live your life.

I have been there before and be aware that as you decide to be yourself, the feeling of fear may try to take you hostage. The voice in your head may say, "What will other people think," "How will they feel," "What will they say," or "You need to stop causing problems." Remember, succumbing to those thoughts only leads you back to the place of pleasing people.

But pause and take a breath; it's okay; all is well. It is not your responsibility to own what other people say, think, or feel. It's only your responsibility to develop, expand, grow, and move forward in your life. You are only responsible for what you say, think or feel. You owe it to yourself to be authentic, to be truthful, to be yourself.

As you overcome challenges and experience breakthroughs, you will live <u>YOUR</u> life, the life you deserve, the life that leads to peace and freedom.

Yes! You can do this, one step at a time, as you set and reinforce boundaries in your life, while applying the emotional CPR.ed process.

You are capable!

Be brave! What does it look like to be brave?

Have courage! What does it require of you to have courage?

Come on! Picture yourself being brave and courageous as you discover your identity. Go ahead, use your voice tactfully, respectfully and responsibly, as you stand in your truth. I have done so and have witnessed others who I work with do the same. Get ready to burst out of your boxes like five bolts of lightning, striking back-to-back as it hits land.

Don't Walk Alone

As you journey and explore the question, "Who Am I?" don't walk alone, nor isolate yourself. I've learned that choosing the right family member, friend, or other people you trust, can serve to be good supporters during your self-discovery journey. Don't be ashamed to connect with a mentor, a coach, or a counselor/therapist. Consider engaging with an accountability partner, pastor, spiritual director or spiritual leader to support you as well.

Along my journey, I have had them all, the journey is not meant to be walked alone. I am VERY appreciative of my counselor, who supported me through applying my own emotional CPR.ed process to my life. The freedom I experienced while she helped me to navigate through unprocessed trauma and experiences using the Eye Movement Desensitization and Reprocessing process (EMDR). I even participated in a Step Study and large/small groups with Celebrate Recovery.

Gesh! Talking about toiling through MANY emotions and dealing with realities while sinking to the bottom of the ocean but then popping back to the top of the water if freeing. The CPR.ed process supported me to stand face to face with me. To feel all my emotions, I allow them to wash over me before I make sound decisions. It takes time! I am cheering you on to stick with it, the result is freedom to thrive in life.

If you can attend workshops, conferences, camps, or other gatherings, do so. Also, read books or listen to helpful podcasts. Doing so will support you as you become self-aware, learn new skills, and navigate your new path along your self-discovery journey.

It's Your Time

Yes! It's YOUR time!

It's YOUR time to be bold, bright, and big. It's time to make decisions for you as you take one step at a time while moving upward, forward, and onward. Say it with me, "It's my time".

Let's go!!

It's YOUR time to gain clarity, understand purpose (or the why), and live-in reality. You get to own and manage your emotions as you make wise decisions for your life.

It's YOUR time to explore, manage, and orchestrate the historical and generational patterns, traditions and expectations of others in your life. Go ahead; take the time to peek into the historical and generational forces of the box of race, family, roles, and religion, or any other boxes self-identified. The time is now! Doing so will provide you with an understanding and insight into how these boxes impact you, your thoughts, feelings, behaviors, and decisions. The boxes impact your WHOLE life.

It's YOUR time to take a moment for yourself, be yourself, hold a space for yourself, and, for once, take care of yourself and your needs. It's okay to embrace ALL parts of yourself, "the good, the bad, and the ugly," and the "great" as society would say. All your life experiences have shaped you and play a role in your journey. You have had absolutely no control over some of your experiences; and at other times, you did have control. In either case, you get to decide where you go from here and how you live your life moving forward. You're responsible for recovering, for healing and to correcting courses.

Who is the owner of your life? You are! Who is the captain of your ship? You are! How cool!

I invite you to embrace the freedom to simply be authentic, to be truthful first to yourself and then to others. Reflect on your experiences from various perspectives, considering all sides of the story. Observe how things change when you recognize the boxes you've been placed into, the ones you've put yourself into, and the boxes you have placed other people into, and expected them to "respond accordingly.

Get ready, make yourself comfortable, perhaps with some soft music and a snack, and prepare to embark on a journey of self-discovery as you explore the question, "Who am I?"

Picture what it's like to live <u>YOUR</u> life. How would it feel to choose and decide to live outside of predefined boxes? As you continue reading, you'll encounter questions throughout the book. Take time to ponder the questions presented as you explore how they relate to your own life experiences.

This journey is all about <u>YOU</u>! After you complete reading this book and begin your journey of transitioning to be your best self, to be truthful, and live your life authentically, I would be delighted to hear about your experiences. Contact me at info@kdtglobalconsulting.com and share your experience. Or you can visit www.kdtglobalconsulting.com to share your experience of your very own Awakening moment along your self-discovery journey.

No more dimming your light! No small playing!

Let's get started as experience how to apply the CPR.ed process as you Identity ReSet 1: The Awakening: WAKE UP!

Identity ReSet 1:

The Awakening: WAKE UP

The Awakening: WAKE UP!

WAKE UP!

Not living YOUR OWN life while striving to live out historical and generational patterns, traditions, and expectations of others, can confine you into boxes and choke the life out of you. Being trapped in boxes often leads to misery, unhappiness, anger, hopelessness, anxiety, depression, or other mental health concerns. Why? Because in the process of conforming and aligning yourself inside of boxes, you gradually lose pieces of your true self.

On the other hand, making wise decisions that align with your purpose, values, and who you are, can bring a sense of calmness, happiness, joy, solitude and peace. Owning your own decisions allows you to learn, grow, thrive in life, and experience true freedom.

Before we delve into each specific box we will discuss (remember, there are many others), I invite you to read about my self-discovery journey of self-discovery and how my awakening experience torpedoed me to shift and take off like a rocket ship heading to explore new things. This shift empowered me to live my life courageously and embrace freedom.

Let's dive into an example of how to apply the CRP.ed process. You'll learn how to as you observe how I navigated the transformation process of my self-discovery. Along the way, I paused to participate in counseling, to receive support from a life coach as I took small, steady steps out of my boxes. My moment of awakening freed me from historical and generational patterns, traditions and expectations of others. I encourage you to discover the exhilaration of waking up and being authentic, and true to who you are.

It's YOUR TIME!

How It All Unfolded

It all began with a HUGE life altering transition as I relocated from Chicago to Las Vegas. Imagine this, imagine being uprooted from EVERYTHING you have ever known since birth (i.e. people, food, yearly seasons, traditions, etc). I was disconnected from all things familiar to me. Although it was a journey I agreed to take, this relocation provided me with a perfect opportunity for soul searching.

A second pivotal moment occurred at work while I was in a group with my team. My director gave me a strange, confused look and asked, "Karen, where do your behaviors come from?" That question hit me like a ton of bricks. I was left stumped, without an answer, and with a question that sparked my curiosity.

The third shift unfolded during a coaching course I attended to become a certified life coach. I expected to gain skills and knowledge to support my teaching and coaching. Little did I know I would gain not just skills and knowledge on how to coach others, I also gained insight, clarity, and understanding of why I think the way I think, why I feel the way I feel and why I behave the way I do. During the course, I began to think, "It's my time, my time to begin connecting with who I am."

One day in class, my awakening moment happened during a 15-minute demonstration. The facilitator said, "I need a volunteer for a demonstration." I hesitated before responding, as my box of religion and family taught me to be "humble"—humble to the tune to not speak, to be silent, to not be seen, and to let others go first. But after no one else volunteered, I slowly raised my hand and said, "I'll do it; I'll volunteer."

The facilitator immediately smiled and said, "Great." I thought, "Oh my, here I go." She continued, "Thank you for volunteering; feel free to discontinue participating at any time." That's when I took a DEEP breath and thought, "Oh my goodness, Karen, what are you doing?" But driven by my usual curiosity, I reasoned with myself, "She did ask for volunteers, so why not me? What could go wrong?"

Everything was going fine until she began asking about my feelings. What? That's where my emotional CPR.ed process began. Instantly, my face turned stone cold, and my heart raced like a herd of horses in the Kentucky Derby. It felt as if a John Deere tractor was lying on my chest.

First, I thought, "Did she just ask me to connect with my feelings and emotions?" "Doesn't she know this is not acceptable?"

In my world, a limiting message I received from my box of race, family, roles, and religion was to "be strong." Being strong equated to stuffing feelings and emotions deep into a backpack. When that backpack got full, then feelings and emotions were transferred into a luggage, then into another larger luggage, followed by stuffing feelings and emotions into a HUGE hope chest. But this only worked for a moment. After stuffing my feelings, I found myself not being able to take the pressure, and as a result, I would explode, like a 23,000-foot-high volcano, because I was no longer "strong."

Oh boy, did I feel pressure during my time volunteering! But something was different this time; I didn't explode. Nor did I hit the "I no longer want to participate" button. Why? Because I was curious about what was taking place inside my inner being. I decided to not hit the reset button instead and instead explore what was the root cause of my thoughts, feelings and behaviors.

As the facilitator continued to ask questions, my responses uncovered that I tend to be controlling, not very flexible and functioned as a perfectionist. Really? Lady! How in the world did we get here? Everyone else in my world knew I had controlling and non-flexible tendencies, and that I was a perfectionist, however, I was in DENIAL. But I began to gain clarity about who I am as I was confronted with the "R" in the emotional CPR.ed process —reality; I had to stand face to face with some realities in my life.

Next, we discussed what contributed to how I became rigid (this is the “P,” for purpose, in the emotional CPR.ed process) and this contributed to my very LOW tolerance for foolishness. Experiencing rigidity within my legalistic box of religion explains the root of my behavior to not be flexible.

“What in the world is this? Who have I become?

She took me back to reflect on my younger years of my life. I really believe she forgot we were in class because she continued to ask questions about my emotions and personal business in the open, in public. This is not acceptable because I don’t discuss my business outside my house. Who can relate to the expectation that you better not talk to anyone or say a thing about what happens inside your house?

Let me hear it! “What goes on in this house stays in this house!” If you don’t relate, what was your experience regarding sharing your “personal business?” I was tempted to yell at the facilitator, “Uh, Ms. Facilitator, aren’t you aware that my race box and family box forbids discussing personal business publicly? This is a generational and historical golden rule and expectations of others. “Come on, lady, get with the program.”

But she didn’t stop there; she persisted, asking more probing questions and delving deeper. This led us to discuss my frustration with people asking for forgiveness when they should have sought permission from the beginning of a situation. This behavior, which I view as foolishness, along with my impatience for dishonesty, lack of authenticity, and unkept promises, began to surface.

Again, I wanted to press the metaphorical “stop, I no longer want to participate” button, like someone hitting the buzzer on the game show, Family Feud, but I couldn’t. The more I answered questions, the more curious I became. The more curious I became, the more comfortable I was digging deeper to be honest with myself, despite my feelings and emotions. The environment was welcoming since I didn’t know anyone in the room. There was no one present to silence me, muzzle me, nor tell me, “Karen be quiet.”

Who else has experienced being silenced or muzzled?

What is it like for you to speak freely?

Although my experience while volunteering was emotional and challenging, I began to be honest with myself. My honesty led to questions about my feelings in the moment which were feeling, let down, hurt, and disappointment. There it was, the emotional CPR.ed process in full force. Clarity continued to flow as I explored possible reasons for my behavior that impacts who I am today. The "why" (purpose) underneath my behavior is a direct result of patterns and experiences that have shaped who I am today.

Facing reality was HARD; it forced me to confront reality and move out of denial. I gleaned insight into why I built walls 12 feet high and 5 feet wide walls in my life to keep me safe. Little did I know, these same walls that protected me also prevented me from connecting with others, building relationships, and stepping out of my comfort zone to thrive in a life. I realized that I must be willing to start dismantling the walls, one brick at a time.

What walls do you need to start dismantling in your life?

She then asked me to stretch out my arms in front of me, with my hands facing each other, and to bring my fingers together to form the shape of a box. Then, she instructed me to bend over into my lap through my hands. I looked at her as if she had lost her mind. I checked the time on my watch (there was still a lot of time left), hesitated, took a deep breath, as I thought, "This woman must be joking." I wanted to tell her, "I'm done." However, despite my feelings, emotions and doing a lot of work, it felt REALLY good to finally share my true thoughts.

I began to feel lighter, as if a load was being lifted off me. I began to feel less intimidated and enjoyed the feeling of freedom wrapping its arms around me, tightly, as if I was a huge cuddly teddy bear. No one was present to reinforce the limiting message to "Be quiet, don't rock the boat," Be seen and not heard," or "to keep the peace."

Does any of these messages ring a bell for you? If they don't, what limiting messages have you heard that left you frozen, stuck, or uncomfortable?

Well, I had already traveled too far in the process of stopping; the self-discovery process was enlightening. Gaining clarity and understanding some realities in my life, in a short period of time left me curious and wanting more. My inner girl just wanted to get it all out. Because, FINALLY, someone was willing to listen to me, to hear what I had to say. In that moment, I was important, I mattered, and I had a voice.

The facilitator continued to guide me through the volunteer process as I was tightly rolled up inside my box, with my head snuggly tucked into my arms, with my face buried in my lap. I literally felt the sensation of being squished and smothered while choking. As we talked, tears started flowing down my face like the cascading waters of Niagara Falls.

Who has experienced tears streaming down your face like a thunderstorm? Who has held back tears while dismissing your feelings and emotions? Remember, tears are cleansing and bring relief, therefore, I invite you to allow tears in your life to flow.

Let's pause for a moment. Think about the boxes in your life. What messages have they conveyed to you?

For me, the boxes delivered limiting messages like, "Karen, be quiet," "Karen, you can't say that" or "You can't do that." "Karen, do the right thing; say the right thing," "now you know that's not right," or "Karen, just leave it alone." These messages also included, "You think you are better than," "Don't you go stirring up trouble," or "Why do you always have to be different?"

Confronted with the question, "Who am I?" I gained clarity. I don't just stir things up, and it's okay to be different. There is nothing wrong with being different. One thought or way is not right, and the other wrong, it's just different. I realized I am someone who asks "why," from a genuine desire to understand, especially when there's a discrepancy or when things are unclear. I am a logical and methodical person who asks questions after listening, observing, and drawing conclusions to gain knowledge and understanding (purpose). My reality is that I am not defiant, nor a rebel, and instead, I am just curious.

What limiting messages from your boxes have influenced who you are today?

As I acknowledged patterns and past experiences, I noticed that when I speak, my tone is very soft, almost like a whisper, after learning to remain silent. Other times, I experience anxiety and there's a lump in my throat, the size of an orange, followed by the feeling of a heavy as a 5-ton weight on my chest.

Am I not important? Yes, I am! Do I matter? Absolutely! Does what I say mean anything? Yes, it certainly does!

But as a result to the patterns, traditions, expectations of others, and historical and generational norms, I grew accustomed to believing limiting beliefs like, "That's just the way it is," "It is what it is," "Because we've always done it this way," and "Why change it?" followed by "Get with the program Karen."

Who wants to constantly fight or be shut down and silenced? Not me, and I'm sure not you either. It's physically, emotionally, and mentally draining.

How does it feel to fight to speak, fight to be heard, or fight to be seen? Being the youngest child, my roles box shaped me to fight to speak, hear and be seen. If you don't have to fight, how do you freely express yourself without limitations?

Instead of fighting, I learned to fly under the radar, falsely comply, "keep the peace," and "go along to get along." I began wearing a mask, ensuring it was appealing and cute. I could have won an Emmy for "Staying in the Background" and an Oscar for "Just Sucking It Up," while losing pieces of myself over time. So, the opportunity to explore these constricting boxes was long overdue and much needed. I experienced an epiphany while speaking about my truth. I realized I turned a blind eye to many things, as my voice gradually silenced over the years, while losing fragments of me year, after year, after year.

What pieces of yourself have you lost? What would it take to begin putting the pieces back together? If you haven't lost any pieces of yourself, what have you done to keep your pieces together?

Though it was challenging to feel while being still rolled up in a box, shifts continued to take place during my awakening of self-discovery. I often would say, "Something is missing in my life." But, thanks to being courageous to step outside of myself and volunteer. This caused the initial heaviness I carried for years, to begin to SLOWLY loosen, leaving me feeling lighter.

Finally! I was able to hear my own voice and listen to my heart. I was able to silence the limiting messages of the historical and generational forces that choked life out of me. It was my time! My time to explore how I needed to undo who I had become.

This time, there were no barriers, no jail bars, no limitations, and no one present telling me, "Don't say that" "No," "Stop," or "Don't do that," and "Don't think that." For once in my life, FINALLY, it was about ME! She wanted to hear what I had to say. I was given permission to be real, authentic, and honest. During this opportunity, I got to be myself and not wear a mask.

Come on, join me, what are three words to describe how it feels for you not to wear a mask?

The facilitator welcomed me to speak freely, and I connected with my voice. The focus was on me, and it was about my life, about "Who I am," instead of my race, family, roles and religion boxes narrating my thoughts. For once in my lifetime, I was able to recognize the value of and the need for me to deal with "MY STUFF" for a change. Wow, the relaxing feelings and emotions that flooded my heart, knowing I was ONLY responsible to hold, deal with my feelings and emotions and not have to manage someone else's stuff.

What would an opportunity like this look like for you?

As I embraced reality, I wasn't obligated to "go along to get along" nor participate in "group think" without taking historical and generational expectations into consideration. Most importantly, I was able to experience this moment WITHOUT JUDGEMENT and fear. While experiencing this freedom, I felt as if I wanted to stand on a stage and wave at everyone in the audience as I smiled with joy while taking a moment to shift from a fixed mindset to a growth mindset. Through the tears of my "Awakening" experience, the process was cleansing and I got to hit the reset button as begin to rethink things.

How would a moment like that feel for you?

At the end of my volunteer process, I sat up, unfolded my hands, and declared, "I don't like being in boxes." On the outside, I may have looked like a hot mess, but I didn't care. Inside, I felt liberated. As I wiped away tears, the tissue clung to my face like old gum on a sidewalk. Part of me felt embarrassed and the other part me didn't care. The sensation of amazement allowed my fragile and vulnerable soul to just be. I had finally embarked on my new journey of freedom.

This led me to a pivotal moment in my life when I hit the reset button opposed to the shutdown button. During the emotional CPR.ed process, I gained clarity and began to understand some things (purpose/why) about myself while confronting reality that I had lost a piece of myself. I navigated through a myriad of emotions, which allowed me to clear my mind and start making decisions for myself.

What decisions do you need to make? What historical and generational patterns, traditions and expectations of others are strangling you like a person holding tight to one million dollars and not letting go? The first decision I made was to begin to peek into my boxes in preparation for me to step out of them.

What does this mean to you?

It means you can do the same as you manage your emotions, stand in your truth, confront reality, and make wise decisions for yourself. Dealing with emotions is an unavoidable part of the process. It's not wise to make decisions when engulfed in emotions, whether negative feelings and emotions, such as anger and sadness, or positive feelings and emotions such as surprise and excitement. You need to navigate through emotions and make rational and wise decisions.

I decided, right there at the end of the volunteer process, that I would no longer be held captive by the boxes of race, family, roles, or religion. I decided that it was time for me. I began a journey not only to survive in life but to thrive.

And you can, too!

From Limiting Messages to Limitless Freedom

As I reflected, that was a LONG 15-minute experience. I recall that at the end, the room was so quiet you could hear a stick pin drop on cotton. But my peers were so kind and gentle as they held a warm and welcoming space for me. We all paused as I got myself together. Then, each person took turns affirming and encouraging me. "Karen, you are brave." "You are courageous." "Karen, you are resilient." We all need people in our lives to affirm and encourage us to be our best.

Who will be your support person as you experience an awakening moment?

I offer to take a moment as you start your self-discovery to affirm and encourage yourself. Say, "I am ________" (fill in the blank)! Say it one more time, "I am ________" (fill in the blank)! Again, a third time, as you begin to walk in freedom, "I am ________" (fill in the blank)!

That brief experience provided me with the opportunity to start some much-needed work in my life. Doing this work was long overdue. Now, you have the chance to disconnect from what everybody says and thinks. What a privilege for you to begin breaking free from your boxes, limiting messages, and historical and generational bondage. How liberating it is to break free from people, places, and things, from people-pleasing, group thinking and having a faulty mindset!

After the course, I continued to unpack my backpack of emotions—hurt, shame, blame, and pain. In doing so, I began to undo who I had become, to start being who I've always been. I needed to keep working to discover my identity, to find out who I am, who I really am. I now laugh at myself as I reflect on how that experience was a priceless 15 minutes of my life.

Following this experience, I didn't stop, I kept going. Over the next two years, as I engaged in counseling, Step Study with Celebrate Recovery as well as large/small groups, bit by bit, I began to crawl out and break free from the suffocating, choking, and limiting boxes. The time had finally come for me as I unraveled the tightly woven baskets and untangled the

HUGE spool of yarn of historical and generational patterns that shaped me and currently impacted me today.

Understand that it will take you time to answer the question, "Who am I?" As you explore and discover who you are, remain focused on your goal to experience limitless freedom as you manage your life and leave a legacy for the next generation.

You no longer must conform to the "status quo," hide your feelings or wear a mask. You don't have to adapt to, be responsible for, own other people's opinions or decisions, carry their feelings and emotions, nor have them to live their lives through you. Despite the feelings and emotions, regardless of anxiety you may feel during your journey, press through and keep going. Being yourself and living your life is indescribable.

Exploring your historical and generational patterns, traditions, and expectations is crucial. It's important for you to decide what you want to continue in your life, what you don't want to continue, and how things might look different to you. As you honor yourself and your values, it's okay to make changes that differ from the behaviors and expectations of others from within your boxes. Whatever decisions you make while exploring the question, "Who Am I," ensure they are your own. Discovering who you are is a journey, not a destination.

How will you manage through not getting sucked back into any of your boxes?

Will some relationships change or shift as you discover your identity and be who you are? Yes, they will.

Will some relationships end? Yes, they will.

In either case, take time to pause, own, embrace, and manage your emotions during the process. As you shift, be true to yourself and make wise decisions, keeping the end goal of freedom in mind.

As you face reality, be authentic, and speak your truth, it may feel like opening a can of worms. When this happened to me, I wanted to stuff the worms back into the can. The worms were slimy and messy, just like the transition and transformational process of self-discovery. Don't try to stuff the worms back into the can. Let out whatever needs to come out. Doing so will not only help you get out of your boxes, but it will also stop the merry-go-round and allow you to get off and stop turning in circles.

What merry-go-rounds will you commit to getting off to begin a new legacy for the next generation?

As you read each chapter, lean in and ponder the MANY questions I had to answer during my self-discovery journey. Ask yourself, "What's next?" "Where do I go from here?" Don't worry about what others think, whether they will like you or align with the decisions you make. Yes! It's SCARY! And although SCARY, confronting the reality of your answers will result in you being authentic, true to yourself, and to be free from people pleasing.

Give yourself permission to sit with and through being honest, vulnerable, and transparent as you use your voice and share from your heart. Again, this allows you to shift from a fixed mindset to a growth mindset. Embrace courage as you set and implement boundaries in your life. Walking in freedom resembles an excited child at their birthday party, running from gift to gift, eagerly tearing off the wrapping paper to see what's inside.

What does limitless freedom look like for you?

Get ready to hit the reset button. Let's get started as you dive into the race and explore the impact race has had on your thinking, feeling and behavior.

No more status quo! No more denial!

Prepare to get out of these boxes you've identified as you explore Identity ReSet 2: Race (or Culture): Really?

Identity ReSet 2: Race (or Culture): WHO SAID SO?

Race (or Culture): Really?

My Foundation and Where It All Began

Your past experiences shape who you are today. I am an African American woman who was raised in an African American community on the south side of Chicago, in the United States. Growing up I attended an all-black church, elementary school, and high school. Although I was exposed to other races, nationalities, and cultures, I didn't experience cohabitating with people of different races daily until my college years.

Both my paternal and maternal families are from Mississippi. I had 20 paternal aunts and uncles, and 13 maternal aunts and uncles because my family is blended. My aunts and uncles have an average of five children each, with some having only one child and others having up to ten.

My introduction and early memories of race, racism, and differences in the world began as I listened to MANY stories and observed various situations as a young child. You see, my family migrated to the North and every summer, I visited Mississippi in the South. There was a significant difference in experiencing race between the North and the South.

What's been your experience in understanding the differences between races?

I come from a family of hard workers. The responsibilities of both my grandfathers were to work and provide for their families, while both of my grandmothers were tasked with caring for the children and the home. We'll revisit this deep-rooted expectation of the roles of males and females later when we discuss the family box.

Times were hard for blacks living in Mississippi during the 40s, 50s, and 60s; as many of them resided on plantations. This situation significantly impacted my family. There were many challenges, but my family was strong and resilient.

My family made a living by working the fields and picking cotton. I recall hearing stories of even children, both old and young, working in the fields, picking cotton. The stories are still vivid about how blacks walked miles to attend schools that were separate from white schools and separate does not mean equal.

My experience of living up North and visiting the South frequently gave me the opportunity to learn about differences and how things were unfair between blacks and whites. Some of the most significant differences were not only between the North and the South but also within the black community in the North. It's one thing to read and hear about racial differences; it's another to see and experience it firsthand.

What's your experience with differences between races?

Messages about Race

I often hear many stories about Mr. Z — that's what I'll call him. For a while, I was confused about how he was a family member. I never met him, nor did he participate in family dinners, reunions, weddings, funerals or other gatherings, nor did he visit anyone. Year after year, I struggled to make the connection between who Mr. Z was and what lineage he belonged to.

As a child, I wondered why someone didn't put Mr. Z in his place or say anything to him. I pondered who left him to be the boss, especially since he wasn't even part of our family. This made me angry.

Accepting the reality that my family experienced oppression and had to ask Mr. Z for "permission" provided clarity of how historical and generational patterns, mindsets, and behaviors become present-day expectations, such as "You can't," "No, Be Quiet," and "Work harder." These limiting messages and others provided a fixed mindset that I am "less than." We'll visit and discuss other limiting messages soon.

As I grew older and put the pieces together, I discovered he wasn't part of my paternal or maternal family. Mr. Z was a sharecropper who owned the land and homes where my family lived. My family reportedly had to ask "permission" from Mr. Z for everything — to buy things, to do things, to be, and unfortunately, how to exist. Interestingly, Mr. Z was a mystery man to me and a crazy as it sounds, he was already deceased long before I was born. But through hearing continuous stories, he was kept very much alive in my mind, and this impact caused me to experience racial and generational trauma.

What does this mean to you?

It means you will be impacted by race while hearing about the experiences and perspectives of previous and current generations. These experiences shape who you are and how you view the world. Although you have become who you are, this is not always representative of who you really are. It also means that sometimes, you accept other people's experiences as your own after hearing about and/or observing their experiences. This is known as secondary traumatic stress (STS).

As I continue to experience secondary traumatic and generational trauma, I remember hearing about a female family member purchasing a car and a male family member asking her, "Did you ask your husband before you made your purchase." This is a perfect example of how people are stuck with fixed mindsets from the past.

What are your fixed mindsets?

What secondary traumatic stress have you experienced?

Sadness and anger crept in as I repeatedly listened to how one of my uncles was reportedly killed at a young age by a white man. Hearing how it happened, how the injustice was handled, and the impact it had on my family was challenging for me. As a child, I wondered why someone didn't put Mr. Z in his place or say anything to him. I pondered who left him to be the boss, especially since he wasn't even part of our family. This made me angry.

Accepting the reality that my family was oppressed and had to ask Mr. Z for "permission" provided clarity of how historical and generational patterns, mindsets, and behaviors become present-day expectations, such as "You can't," "No, be quiet," and "Work harder." These limiting messages and others provided a mindset that you are "less than." We'll visit and discuss other limiting messages soon. This shaped how I viewed the world.

Living in the North, I understood "the process" to be that when someone was killed, the police were called, and the situation was properly handled. That was my perception as a child. I didn't understand why nothing was done about the man who was said to have killed my uncle. Many questions ran through my mind like rain coming down in a thunderstorm, such as, "Who did anything about this?" "How was this injustice allowed to happen? But, as I grew older, I came to understand the "process" was not fair in the North nor in the South.

That wasn't the only difference between the North and the South—there were many. The homes in the South didn't look the same as those in the North. Northern homes were often made of brick and were larger. In contrast, in the South, the homes of black families were smaller, worn down, with dingy, dirty white or chipping paint. Some homes were not leveled and instead leaning instead. Some lacked a screen door; if they had one, it was raggedy and falling apart. But the homes white people lived in were lavish and looked completely different.

I remember watching family members boil water to wash dishes and clothes. The unforgettable experience of trudging through the woods to use the bathroom in the outhouse clearly stands out to me. It was a journey to get to the outhouse, with the dirt clinging to my feet like a shell on a hard-boiled egg. The smell of the woods, coupled with the scent of the farm animals (specifically the hog pen), was strong. Flies swarmed the outhouse, making me second guess if I really needed to use it.

Thankfully, I was relieved to return to my aunt's home, there was a bathroom and running water on the inside of the house. We stayed with her each time we visited Mississippi. Her home was different; it was built with brick, like other homes in the North.

I had so many questions racing through my mind like a 12-mile marathon. How did we get here? Why were there such vast differences between the North and the South? Why weren't the roads paved in Mississippi like they were in Chicago? Why was the dirt a different color in the South? And the mosquitoes were different too. Their bites from the mosquitoes in the South would leave you with huge lumps and bruise for days.

What was your introduction to the differences between races?

As a child, an interesting and VERY bizarre thing that troubled me was that no one ever spoke about these differences. Why? This question lingered in my thoughts repeatedly. Was I the only one seeing what was happening? Gradually, I began to accept all the racial differences as "normal." This adaptation shaped who I became. For example, I learned not to speak about certain things nor address things that are clearly happening. But deep down, I didn't believe it at all. It wasn't normal or acceptable to me, both as a child and as an adult. But now, I have courage and a motto to "Let's Talk About It."

I didn't fully understand the whole "race" situation. The limiting messages and expectations of others seeped into my fragile, vulnerable, and innocent mind like crackers or bread soaking up broth in a bowl of soup. Unbeknownst to me, my mindset, life and identity were being shaped. My view and perspective of the world were developing as my race box was being created. Your box of race was created for you, too.

What does the box of race that was created for you look like?

How has it changed?

How has it remained the same?

What needs to change for you?

We are all shaped by what is ingrained in us about race. The messages we receive are sometimes direct, and at times, they are indirect or subtle. Limiting messages about race and culture not only shapes our identity but also impacts on how we make decisions and how we live our life every day. As we discuss limiting messages and fixed mindsets, keep in mind messages are not only isolated to race box; they may also be present in other boxes in our lives. We'll discuss two limiting messages I experienced about race.

Limiting Messages

The first limiting message we'll explore is the notion that "You Can't" "You Should" or "You shouldn't." After repeatedly hearing these messages, I began living my life with limitations. The limiting messages instilled in me a sense of fear and paralysis, and it also impacted on my confidence and boldness. During my journey with others I teach and coach, I've observed many others who are fearful, live their lives frozen or stuck and lack the confidence to take a different step forward.

The second limiting message is, "You have to do more," "Be more," and "Be better than," to prove you can and that you are qualified. Living my life from these positions turned me into a perfectionist, constantly striving to meet and exceed historical and generational traditions, patterns and expectations of others just to have a seat at the table.

What limiting messages have you received?

What messages have you received that created a sense of inferiority or superiority for you?

While engaging in counseling, I had to distinguish between who I have become and who I am. I was stuck in the box of race and had to manage my emotions while doing the work to understand how race and culture have impacted and shaped me.

My counselor was instrumental in guiding me through the raging waters as I worked to get out of the box of race (and other boxes also) as I journeyed through the Eye Movement Desensitization and Reprocessing (EMDR). The box was smothering me like a tightly rolled sleeping bag. I had to confront heart-wrenching realities as I gained clarity about my truth after being taken hostage by someone else's experience that had become my own. I had to face hard truths about how my experiences over time controlled me and shaped my fixed mindset. You, too, must clarify how your experiences hijack your emotions, how your emotions influence your thoughts, how your thoughts dictate your behavior and how you show up to live your day-to-day and make decisions.

Reflecting on my experiences because of the color of my skin, caused me to accept the reality that I wasn't okay. Despite "being strong, picking myself up, dusting myself off, and continuing to move forward. Although my family taught me how to be resilient and perseverance, there were still aspects of my experience with race that were frustrating, disappointing, painful and hurtful.

What does it feel like to think you're okay to later admit that you're not?

I had to confront the chilling reality as I gained clarity that I was stuck in some areas of my life due to secondary traumatic stress and generational trauma. This realization rocked my world and runs deep and wide, just as the five great lakes that connect the Midwest of the United States. I was a mess during counseling as I connected, admitted and looked at my unprocessed trauma and experiences in the face as I walked my self-discovery journey.

However, I was determined to navigate the tides, to work diligently to overcome my trauma and the limiting messages that were baked on me like toothpaste on a toothbrush. I needed to become the boss of my life rather than allowing someone else's experience, trauma and limiting messages to dictate my life. I had to weather through the tornado of emotions. This allowed me to shift from a fixed mindset to a growth mindset.

After applying the emotional CPR.ed process, I continued to gain clarity about who I am as I began to understand situations (purpose) and dealt with MANY uncomfortable realities. Another hard realization I faced was I unconsciously passed some of the limiting messages, fixed mindsets and generational racial trauma to my children. This not only grieved me as I managed my emotions, but it also forced me to quickly reassess myself, and make the decision to course-correct, and to rectify unsound information I held them accountable to uphold. I had to set aside pride as I admitted, "Mommy was wrong," and provide them a better way and various perspectives about life when it comes to race. It was time for me to hit the reset button.

Let's look deeper and into more detail, the limiting messages that shaped me, that shaped who I am and formed my identity.

Limiting Messages: "You Can't," "You Should," "You Shouldn't"

It was 1983 when Harold Washington became the first black Mayor of Chicago after winning against a white woman, Jane Byrne. Keep in mind Chicago was incorporated in 1837 by Jean Baptiste Point du Sable, a black man. With this, there were 146 years of differences, discrimination, and oppression of blacks before Chicago had a black mayor. At the time of this win, as a little girl, I didn't understand the weight of having a black mayor. I didn't really understand the depth of this being "a BIG thing." Later, I came to understand what a great victory it was for Harold Washington, for black, for people of color and for the city.

I was sitting in school when my 3rd-grade teacher made the announcement. She turned on a small radio, and there was a lot of celebration. She opened the classroom door and greeted other teachers, as they cheered and hugged each other. So, what did my peers and I do? We celebrated too.

After hearing about Harold Washington, "the first black Mayor," I asked, "Why hasn't there been a black Mayor before?" Yes, I was taught history about blacks and whites. But reading and knowing about history is different from experiencing it. After I asked the question, my teacher's smile turned upside down, as she tilted her head and kindly replied, "Blacks weren't allowed to hold positions."

As I walked home from school, the atmosphere was full of celebration, with people cheering and horns honking. Later evening, the phone at my home rang continuously as people called to talk about and celebrate the huge win for blacks in Chicago.

Later, I asked again, "Why were blacks not allowed to hold the position of Mayor?" I received "the look" and was told, "Go sit down."

This was another deposit into my innocent vulnerable soul. I had another shaping experience about my world view regarding race, racism and inequities. And yes, I was taught about world history, listened to others, and watched many documentaries. But as a little girl, again, my mind couldn't fully comprehend all that was happening. I knew something significant was occurring, but I couldn't fully understand or articulate it.

What is your experience of standing face to face with differences between races?

Another incident occurred around 1987 or 1988 when I was 12 or 13 years old. One Saturday morning, as my friends and I were heading out of the house, my uncle, who was drinking coffee at the kitchen table, stopped us.

Uncle: Where are you going?

Me: To the mall.

Uncle: What mall?

Me: Evergreen Plaza.

His expression changed dramatically, and he asked again, "Where?" When I answered, "Evergreen Plaza," again, oh boy, his reaction was SUPER intense, and it felt like he saw a bear attacking children. He pushed his chair back, placed his coffee cup on the saucer, came closer to my face, and asked again, "WHERE?" Before I could answer, he immediately demanded, "No, you're not going," "You can't go there." I was confused. We lived near 95th and Ashland Avenue, bordering the Longwood community, which is a white community and the mall, Evergreen Plaza, is located on the other side of Longwood. Because my parents had a growth mindset, they often allowed us to visit the mall, sometimes by riding the bus, and other times by walking.

But my uncle, who's mindset was fixed, was adamant as he continuously yelled while telling my mom why she shouldn't allow me to go to the "white mall." It felt like I was run over by a train carrying a ton of cargo, as he exclaimed, "you know we are not welcomed in those places, we're black." This was his truth, not mine, nor my parents. My mouth kept me in trouble, and of course I asked, "Who said we can't go to the malls with white people?" What did I say that for? As he gave me "the look," I remembered the drill, so I remained quiet as my uncle and mom went back and forth with each other, and she eventually told me to leave for the mall.

Each time I was silenced, shut down or muzzled, I lost a piece of myself and became a "quiet person," which is NOT me, at all. I'm naturally outspoken but reluctantly comply to "keep the peace, but I always had thoughts racing through my mind about my truth.

While in counseling as I applied the emotional CPR.ed process, I gained clarity and embraced that I am a thinker and one who processes and requires details and understanding. I learned it's okay to think for myself and ask questions. And I now continue to practice sharing my thoughts, and asking questions, opposed to being silent and shrinking back.

What does this mean to you?

It means it's okay to hit the reset button and unravel who you have become.

But back to the mall situation, as I walked to the mall that day, I pondered, "Who said I can't be with white people?" It was a reality check for me that division lines really do exist. The confusion between growing up in the North in Chicago and visiting the South in Mississippi all came rushing back.

As I continued to sort through situations, the black-and-white differences were stark and unsettling. Emotions overwhelmed me, like a fire hydrant opened for summer fun, flooding the streets with water. Those times were fun until the fire department re-capped the hydrant.

Who had the childhood experience of playing in the water using the opened fire hydrant? If you didn't have this experience, what was your childhood experience while playing in the water?

Returning to the topic, the experience with my uncle reinforced yet another limiting belief in my box of race. My identity shifted, and a piece of me, of Karen, was violently torn away like abruptly ripping a band-aid off.

Fast forward, the limiting belief resurfaced in 2020 when I told my son "You can't go outside to run." You see, he is an avid basketball player, who often runs for exercise or to blow off steam. But during the high racial tensions following the death of George Floyd and the insurrection at the White House, I felt fear. The tensions were higher than the Sears Tower in Chicago or the Empire State Building in New York. The atmosphere was charged with daily riots and unrest.

I found myself feeling choked and then the feeling of anger moved in. What was underneath the anger? Anger is a secondary emotion, it was really guilt, shame, hurt, disappointment, and frustration because I placed a limiting belief on my son. During this time the racial tension was high, especially with us living in a predominantly white community. Not only did I experience painting a limiting message on him and his future of "you can't," unfortunately, regretfully and sadly, I passed the same limiting messages to the next generation.

From his perspective, he simply wanted to go for a jog in the park wearing his jogging suit and hoodie. His doing so in the predominantly white community caused me appropriate concern, as I feared something terrible might happen to him. When I told him "No," he turned to me and asked, "Why not?" Oh my, always curious, asking questions and needing understanding, this sound familiar. He needed an answer and what I provided didn't make sense to him. Yes, he and my daughter are my children, curious, asking questions, needing things to make sense. With this, we are neither rebellious nor rebellious.

As he continued to ask questions, I was immediately transported back to the experience with my uncle, who told me "I couldn't" go past Ashland Avenue to the white mall. It was at that moment that I realized I needed time to apply the emotional CPR.ed process, to further unpack my experiences, and get out of my box of race. I was passing down to the next generation the same patterns and foolishness that I hated, and that hindered me from being me, being free and thriving.

What messages like "You can't," "You should," or "You shouldn't," have you experienced?

What messages have you received that have impacted who you are?

I invite you to open your race box and identify one thing you will commit to do as you take a step out of your box while beginning to arrest your limiting beliefs.

Limiting Message: "Do More" and "Be More"

The message of "Do more" and "Be more," accompanies and supports the need to "prove yourself." There's no need to prove yourself to anyone. Again, this expectation came from watching and hearing stories about my family's experience growing up in the South, in Mississippi, from television, society, etc. These limiting messages also came from watching my parents work harder to provide a better life. I really appreciate my parents. They were intentional to position their children to have better experiences than they had.

My dad was "hard on me" and pushed me to do my best. I now have clarity that he was not "hard on me." I understand the purpose and reason why his expectations were high. My mom would drill into me, "Go to school and get a degree." My reality is they knew what I would face living in a white world while being black. They were preparing and equipping me for life in a broken world, in a racial world.

Reading books is what was required of me while growing up. Not only reading books, but I was also required to read dictionaries and encyclopedias, and I often visited the library. I remember using the Dewey Decimal System to locate books at the library. Little did I know, during that time my dad and mom were expanding my vocabulary, knowledge, and language.

Who remembers encyclopedias? Sometimes I laugh as I reflect and think, "Where in the world was Google back in the day?" And the Dewey Decimal System, who came up with that? People today have no clue how easy they have it with all the technology we have.

Reading and earning all A's in school was the expectation. Anything less than an A earned me a pep talk that began with, "What happened? What's going on with this B?" The pep talk included a walk back to the living room, where the dictionary and encyclopedia sat on a shelf. I'd have to grab a book and go back to the dining room to read for hours. If we didn't have homework, my dad provided us with some, it was reading the dictionary and encyclopedia.

Going to college was an expectation from my parents. "My way to a better life" was getting an education. This is what my dad and mom always drilled into me. My dad would tell me, "You have to work harder and be better than others to survive and make it in this white world." So, that's what I did; I worked harder.

While preparing to attend college, I sought assistance from a well-known person who assisted black youth to obtain scholarships. I inquired of him about attending the University of Illinois at Chicago (UIC), and he told me, "You can't go there; you won't make it." I thought, "Oh my, here we go again with this "You Can't" stuff. He began to share statistics about how many blacks were not successful graduating from UIC. And for those who did, it took them five to six years to complete a four-year program. He continued to repeat, "How hard," I would have to work.

And, of course, Karen had her questions parading in her mind, such as, "According to whom?" and "Why is this so?" I was completely silent, feeling inferior, deflated, and discouraged. I didn't use my voice to share my questions and never returned to meet with him again. Without any help from him, I applied to UIC, was accepted, and enrolled in school. Then, freshman year arrived, and it was not a smooth process at all.

You see, I graduated high school with honors, ranking number four out of more than 300 students in my senior class. I held the office of class secretary and graduated with honors after being a member of the National Honor Society and National Beta Club. I was also highlighted in Who's Who Among High School Students.

I only share this to provide insight into how I excelled academically and was exceptionally prepared for college, or so I thought. Although I was aware of inequities, I quickly learned firsthand and personally that attending an all-black school had not fully prepared me to be academically equipped to align with my peers and counterparts.

My dad was right; I had to work harder. The emotional CPR.ed process supported me in beginning to gain clarity that he wasn't "hard on me." I had to stop being angry with him. The purpose my dad pushed me for is to equip me to conquer and excel in an unfair world. The reality is that my dad loves me, would never do anything to hurt me, and he was helping me.

Thankfully, because of my parents' push, I was prepared to stay in the game and thrive at UIC despite the challenges I faced. I spent countless hours researching and participating in tutoring, just trying to catch up and keep up. It made me feel uneasy as I stood face to face with yet another reality. My reality was that although my primary and secondary education was free, the academics were not and still not equal across races and communities. It was an eye-opener to realize that although I was soaring academically in my black school, I was lagging in some areas compared to students of other races and nationalities within the United States and internationally as well.

"Work harder," they said, and I did just that. I did so not only to achieve and be successful but also "to prove" that I could attend UIC and graduate in four years. Despite being discouraged by that man, I defied his statistics. I graduated from UIC with my bachelor's degree in four years, compared to 5-6 years. Not only did I earn my bachelor's degree in four years, but I also participated in an accelerated program during my undergraduate program and earned my master's degree in one year.

Contrary to man's belief, and despite being black, I graduated in 5 years with two degrees. Yes, I "worked harder" because I chose to and because I had to. Unfortunately, I also worked harder to "prove that man wrong." Because how dare you tell me that "I can't or I won't succeed." I didn't become what "they" said

What message have you received that you defeated and made it into a lie?

The limiting message of "work harder" work ethic didn't end there. I found myself "working harder" as I climbed the leadership ladder in my field, which was primarily dominated by whites. I consistently felt the need to do more to prove myself to people. Let's look forward to today. At times, I still find myself "working harder." Sometimes, I must pause and ask myself, "Am I working hard because that's who I am, or because I choose to, or am I working hard to prove myself?"

What about you?

What are your motives behind why you do what you do?

This drive to "work harder" contributes to my unnecessary urge to "do more," "be more," and exceed expectations. In discovering who I really am, I embrace that I don't have to prove myself. I don't have to be perfect, and I don't have to prove anyone wrong. What's required of me is to just do my best. I don't have to get everything right all the time. Instead of being perfect, I embrace that I have flaws, but still awesome, therefore, I'm flawsome.

Participating in Celebrate Recovery has supported me to be flawsome and challenge limiting messages. What limiting messages have you received that impact who you are? Again, I invite you to open your box of race, identify one thing you must do to take a step out of it, as you hit the reset button.

A Cultural Awakening

Let me share how all of this is relevant to you. Regardless of your race, it's imperative you understand how your experiences with race have shaped you to become who you are. As I processed my experiences and applied the emotional CPR.ed process, I began to become aware of some of the limiting messages that affected me. It has been highlighted that some of the historical and generational patterns, traditions, and expectations exist because of other people's racial experiences. I have decided to make choices for my life and not to continue to own someone else's racial experiences. I am committed to overcoming secondary traumatic stress and generational trauma.

You must recognize that some of your family members embrace their liberties and freedom. These liberties are seen as some of my family members and friends hold the roles of entrepreneurs, school principals, or superintendents. Other roles include supervisors; some have degrees and some don't and are yet still. Some of my family members have worked jobs for over 25-30 years, retiring from positions once deemed "not for us." Despite differences, unfairness, and inequalities, my parents and other family members have paid off homes, and I have had my home built. As you can see, we didn't become what our limiting messages predicted for our lives.

Although there have been successes, I have other family members and friends with fixed mindsets, succumbing to limiting messages. Neither way is right nor wrong; it's just different. People have the right and choice to be wherever they need to be or want to be. As you can see, people have different expectations and perspectives on how they live out their lives. Again, one way is not right, and the other wrong; it's just different. The goal is for you to identify who you are, to make decisions and decide how you live your life, not someone else's.

What limiting messages have you overcome?

What limiting messages have your family overcome?

A New Perspective

Let's take a moment to reflect: Which of your family members are stuck or jailed emotionally or mentally from limiting messages as a result to race or culture?

How has this impacted you?

What unwelcome historical and generational traditions, patterns or expectations of others will you choose not to accept pass on to the next generation?

It's time for you to discover who you really are. Don't let someone else's decision about how they live their life, from a stance of being in the race box, dictate who you are and how you live your life.

Hit the reset button and begin to undo who you have become, to be who you really are. Get out of the box!

Take a moment to explore how to apply the emotional CPR.ed process yourself.

Clarity: Where did your thoughts about race begin?

Purpose: Why are things about race the way they are?

Reality: What do you really believe?

Emotional: As you answer the questions, stay with it, own your feelings without judgement, and don't feel compelled to own or manage other people's feelings.

Decision: What's one more thing you will commit to getting out of your box of race?

Be willing to look at both sides of the coin and view your experience from different perspectives. Remember, it may have appeared that my dad was mean and harsh, but on the flip side, he was concerned about me, and the purpose of pushing me was to prepare me to be successful and thrive in life.

I could have continued to hold onto my perception that my uncle just didn't want me to live my life. But that was not the case. His experiences with race caused him to be fearful, and he projected his fear onto me. I understand the importance of gaining clarity and understanding my why. Unfortunately, my "stuff" became my son's, and my experience (just as my dad's experience of being black in the South) became my parenting style until I decided to do something different.

At the end of the day, although the approaches and responses of my dad and my uncle towards me (and mine towards my son) "were a bit much," this didn't take away from their heartfelt care for me and their commitment to protecting and providing for me. I was right there, too; my heart as a mother is to care for and protect my son and my children, and not to place limitations on them. I had to shift from being mad at my dad and uncle, and forgive them, course correct with my son, and not carry my guilt around in a huge bag big enough for two people. I must not let my experiences overshadow my love for the wonderful people my dad and uncle are to me. I am thankful for both my dad and uncle.

You must sit down and really think about both sides of situations and look at the complete person. Don't condemn them for their approach (although their behavior is not condoned); instead, love them and forgive them. Manage through your emotions, and give people grace, just as others have done for you.

The limiting messages of "you can't," or "you should not," "do more," "be more," and "be better than" may not apply to you. While you address race, identify the messages you have received, and decide what your truth is and how you live your life. For some of you, your messages may be that of superiority. If this is the case, ask yourself "Who am I," "What you really believe.

To all of you, what messages shape your thoughts and feelings and then impact your decisions?

It's time to begin to get out of the race box. It's time for you to make decisions for yourself and not allow the historical and generational expectations of others to impact or interfere with your life. Ensure your choices and decisions align with your values and your truth.

You get to decide how you live your life from a place of freedom. Pause for a moment and reflect on this, "What do you need to do differently?

No more limiting messages! No more fixed mindsets!

Let's continue our journey and peek into the box of family, Identity ReSet 3: Family: Now, Why Do We Do This?

Identity ReSet 3: Family: Now, WHY DO WE DO THIS?

Family: Now, Why Do We Do This?

Getting Centered and Getting Clear

Take a moment to reflect on your own identity; not the identity that belongs to your family, the identity that belongs to YOU. Who are you?

Being a part of a family sometimes breeds "group thinking." Group thinking (be it from family, friends, society, etc.) is not always your way of thinking or what you believe. You will drown slowly, attempting to live up to the historical and generational patterns, traditions, and expectations of others, especially when they don't align with your values and your truth. Standing in truth while honoring your values will enable you to live a fulfilling life.

What generational and historical expectations are you struggling to live up to?

How often do you ask yourself, "Now, why do we do this?" What I've experienced and observed while working with others is that we tend to shrug our shoulders, to go along, to get along. Then, we comply begrudgingly, and this leads us to deal with feelings of anger and/or guilt. Why? Because we didn't speak up or agree to something from a place of emotions of feeling obligated.

We fail to share what we really believe or want, and sometimes, we don't buy into everything that is passed down from generation to generation. What's expected no longer aligns with our expectations. Somehow, we feed into group thinking, agree to what's being said, politely walk away, and then do the complete opposite.

This then positions us to face frustrations later down the road and we must deal with the backlash and chaos from family members while being left to "explain" our actions.

Where have you seen yourself in either place?

You are not alone! Some of you may have experienced the repetitive cycle of living out, adapting to, and tolerating the same historical and generational, patterns, traditions, and expectations of others time and again. Why? The reasons often cited are "that's just what we do," "that's the way we've always done it," or simply "that's just the way it is."

The missing piece leaves you clinging to an overpacked backpack or luggage's of emotions, is that you might not fully understand the 'why' behind your family's group thinking, especially when the reason provided is just "because I said so." At the same time, you might find yourself not speaking up, lacking authenticity, and not standing in your truth as you express your perspective, opinions, values, and needs.

In trying to "comply" or "keep the peace," what you truly believe is often compromised. But what underlies this compliance? Avoidance of confrontation? Not wanting to deal with criticism from family members who may shun or reprimand you, or make you feel guilty because your way of thinking, values, or actions differ from theirs?

What can happen at the end of the day as you comply, avoid, or do not deal with things? You might find yourself giving in, dishonoring your values, and gradually losing pieces of yourself, one piece at a time. However, there is hope. Just as you lost parts of yourself bit by bit, you can also rediscover who you truly are, piece by piece.

Our families are our families. We don't get to choose our family of origin. Keep in mind that ALL families have strengths, assets, and something to offer. At the same time, ALL families are not perfect and have challenges.

As you explore your family box, remember the importance of looking at the entire picture of your family. Oftentimes, we tend to be so hurt or angry about what "didn't go right" or "what's wrong," we fail to see our family for its' wholeness despite the challenges. As you explore your family from all perspectives, you must do the work. You must ask the questions in search of clarity, to understand the purpose, as you stand face to face with your reality. Reality as to what has happened in your family, how it impacts and shapes who you are.

While you seek to understand yourself and your family, I invite you to lean into and manage your emotions in search of the hidden you. This is needed as you examine who you are outside of how you've been shaped, what you've been told, instructed to be, taught, and learned from your family. It's time for you to make decisions.

How have you been shaped by your family?

As you view things from all perspectives, from both sides of the coin, as you explore your experiences and how they have impacted/affected you. Don't only focus only on what didn't happen, what should have or could have happened, the "negative" side of things, also focus on "the positive," what did happen and what went well. Don't get stuck dwelling on unaddressed emotions; instead, have the courage to explore all perspectives. Become curious about how your experiences and emotions have "positively" and "negatively" shaped you.

What have you learned?

How have you grown?

When you look in the mirror, who do you see?

Join me as I share my journey, as I explored my family situations while embracing the "good, the bad, the ugly and the pretty" of my experiences. In doing so, I have given myself permission to have and own my opinions, to critically think for myself, and to explore things from different perspectives as I honor my values. I stand in my truth and make independent decisions, opposed to decisions based on groupthink. Get ready to hit the reset button as you define and connect with who you really are.

Let's get started.

Clearing the Pathway

I love my family tremendously. My paternal and maternal family have been instrumental in laying a strong foundation for my life. Values such as unity, perseverance, caring for others, self-love, and humility have been instilled in me.

As I navigated through life as a young adult, I began to make choices that caused me to hit bumps on the road. Not only did I hit bumps, I also fell into A LOT of huge potholes. The potholes were about the size of a car tire, and some of them were larger than tires on 18-wheeler trucks. These potholes are a result of decisions I made without having clarity and decisions that were entangled in "group thinking." My decisions were aligned with what "I was supposed to do" or aligned with historical and generational patterns, traditions and expectations of others.

Who can relate to this? If you can't, what are other external factors that contribute to the decisions you make?

During my young adult years, my views, perspectives, and opinions were enmeshed (in some cases, overly consumed) with my family's decisions, views, perspectives, and opinions. As I navigated through various encounters and experienced life, it becomes clear that there were puzzle pieces missing. Things were blurred as I experienced challenges and struggled to play in the sandbox in the world with other people.

What have you experienced as you engaged other people whose values, perspectives, and opinions are different from your experience or unfamiliar to you?

How do you manage when things don't happen "the way they are supposed to?"

As things became blurred, it felt like I was constantly "messing up," "fixing" the mess, or re-doing moments in my life. At times, it felt like I was running through my life wildly, just like the seasons of summer, spring, winter, and fall. I was attempting to force the world into my world of historical and generational patterns, traditions, and expectations of others. I wanted everyone to behave and do things "the way my family did," "the way my family behaved," or "the way things were to be done."

As I engaged with other people in life, things had to go "my way" because, of course, I believed my families was "was the right way" or "the only way." I was not willing to listen to anyone outside of my family, again, convinced that my family's way was the "right" way and in some cases, the only way. This rigidity meant I wasn't flexible or receptive to hearing, exploring, knowing, or learning anything different, nor viewing matters from different perspectives.

What was your experience?

My life would shine bright like spring and summer during "good times." However, at other times, I found myself in or even created violent storms through decisions I made. The resulting pain felt like the fierce and brutal winds of Chicago, in the United States. I had been molded and shaped by what worked for my parents, their parents, and previous generations. My brain was clouded as I was exposed to new things in life, and my personal experiences and realities I faced in life, clashed with those of my family.

Who have I become? What do I want? Where is my voice? Who can relate? If not, what has been your experience?

What became truly disturbing is I consciously and unconsciously passed on my family's historical and generational patterns, traditions and expectations of others to my children and other people as well. Some of what I passed on to them was sound and wise. For some of the other things I passed on, I found myself placing my children in the same boxes that I detested. The same boxes I felt suffocated.

As I observed my children struggling in some of the same areas (and different areas, too) that I struggled in as they tried to "fit into" and replicate our family generational mold. As they grew older, they began to gain their own clarity while exploring the "why" beneath their feelings, thoughts, behaviors and perspectives. As they asked me questions, at times, I could not provide them with a response that made sense. The only answer I was able to provide was "because that's the way it is" or "that's the way it's always been done." I really didn't believe any of those explanations, and this forced me to search for the reasons. While doing so, sometimes the reason didn't align with me, or no longer served me and I had to sit and ask myself, "Woman, Karen, what are you doing?

What responses have been provided to you that just don't

make sense?

What things do you question?

What do you really believe?

I had to circle back around to my children and, of course, correct the subjective misinformation I provided to them that came from historical and generational traditions, patterns and expectations of others. For example, there is nothing wrong with having tattoos, and there is nothing wrong with males wearing earrings. It's okay to miss a day of school because life doesn't end when you don't have perfect attendance. I had to share with them that it's okay not to attend a family event, miss a day of worship service, or choose to attend a different church. All these things are subjective and left to the person to make their decision, opposed to group thinking of, "This is what you are supposed to do or not to do."

Expectations of others and patterns are hardwired ways of thinking developed by my family box. I had to apologize to my children for holding them accountable for things that were not "law," and instead were subjective. I then guided them on how to gather information and make decisions for themselves based on facts, their values, and their truth, as opposed to what someone told them, even if it was me, their mom. Even when I disagree with their decisions, it's me who has the responsibility to manage my emotions, as I continue to love them unconditionally and without judgement.

After we acknowledged that by default, chapters of their lives had been written for them, I literally handed them a pen and empowered them to, from this point forward, begin to write the subsequent chapters of their life as they live them out. They aren't responsible for what they experienced, and they are responsible for how they respond and the decisions they make moving forward. They (nor you) are victims and can only control what's in their (your circle of control.

What does this mean to you?

I'm glad you asked. Despite what you've experienced, what's happened to you, been told to you, or passed down to you, those are the beginning chapters of your life that have been written for you. You have the responsibility to be the captain of your ship. And the beauty is, just like my children and those whom I teach and coach, your pen belongs in your hand, as you define who you are while writing your next chapters. You get to do that, not your family box.

I too had to do the same thing, as I found myself asking, "Who am I?" "Who have I become?" I reflect on the question my director asked me one day, "Karen, where does your behavior come from?" Geesh, even now, it makes me shiver to know that I was so disconnected from my inner self and not aware of the patterns of my own behavior. It's amazing how others outside of your world can see you trying to fit a circular peg into a triangular hole, when you can't even see it yourself, and you're the peg.

I wonder, what patterns are you struggling to fit into?

What areas of your life are you wearing a mask?

What do you need to do to live life in an authentic way?

Hit the reset button! Losing who you are, one piece at a time, is no longer an option. It's never too late.

Understanding How Patterns Shape Behavior

What patterns and values have been passed down to you?

My family spends A LOT of time together, and we typically gather every holiday. The value of love and togetherness stems from my forefathers and my family's deep southern roots. We LOVE family gatherings, attending events and doing things together. Over the last few years, as a Cousin's Gathering, we've gathered at Mall of America in

Minnesota and in Detroit Michigan where we visited downtown and Motown. We recently experienced our first family vacation, a cruise to the Bahamas. My great aunt who was 93 joined us and had a great time. Taking cruises and having a passport to travel is a shift for some of my family and shifted patterns on how we travel.

Where did my initial shape begin? From generations of shaping. I am the fifth of five children. My parents have been married for over 50 years, and I grew up in a two-parent, middle-class working family in a house in Brainard Park, on the Southside of Chicago, in the United States – a place I still call home, a place with rich memories. My close-knit family of origin includes my dad (he's my Pappa Bear), my dear mother (she's my Angel), two protective brothers, and two caring sisters. My nephew, who was born when I was eight years old, is more like a brother to me. Hence, he's my "nephew-brother," and he calls me his "auntie-sister." My oldest brother and sister played significant roles in our family, helping my parents with household and childcare responsibilities while my parents worked.

I have fond memories of my cousins sleeping overnight at my house. As we were ONLY allowed sleepovers with family. I also stayed overnight at their house as well. At times, we disagreed on who would stay overnight with who. Our parents did not care; we just needed to figure it out before cars began to pull off.

I have cousins, with whom we grew up together more like siblings. Two of my cousins and I are still like three peas in a pod. Although we are adults now and don't live in the same state, we never miss a beat when we are connected. When we were younger, although they were boys, we would tussle and wrestle. They would "TRY" to run me down, but I hung right in there with them. This is one of the places where I learned to be tough and rough and to stand my ground.

Do you see how something so simple while playing can shape who you are?

They were overprotective (at times more than my brothers), and when I began to date, they would run my male friends away. Even today, they still think they are the boss of me, so I must remind them, "You all cannot treat me like that anymore." Although we tease and pick at each other, we love each other. I know they have my back, and I always have theirs. We always have laughs and there is never a dull moment when we are together. Today, I find myself protective and part of this behavior has been learned from family.

Speaking of fond memories, I also have female cousins who are more like sisters also. We've laugh together, cry together, get spanked together, and stay in trouble together. While on a cruise, my cousin and I got locked out of our cabin as we were minding someone else's business. Despite living in different states, we remain connected via calls, chat groups, etc. as we support each other, and cheer each other on. One phone call is all that is needed, and shortly thereafter, we will all be right there. Again, my behavior of togetherness has stemmed from my family.

My dad provided me with knowledge of how to think "street-smart" (I learned this from other family members as well) and how to live life. My mom provided me with knowledge of how to be a lady and how to be wise as she built a strong spiritual foundation for me. With all of this, I am well-rounded, I guess.

While trying to "figure out who I am," I found myself in places and spaces "in the street" that contradicted my spiritual of my upbringing. Why? Because I was looking for the missing pieces or to fill in the pieces of living in both worlds. And I figured out fast, fast, the "street life," or the "fast life," was not the life for me. Other people, I'm sure, navigate the "street life" and the "fast life" much better than me. And remember, it's one way is not better than or less than; it's just different.

Again, despite how you have been shaped, you must know and do what's best for you. Are we all supposed to continue upholding the same thoughts, feelings, and behaviors, year after year, and pass them down to future generations? No. I struggled with being told "how to live" or "how to be" while observing situations unfold with both my paternal and maternal family where they behaved contrary to what they expected from others. This was confusing and forced me again to take a deep dive into making decisions for myself that aligned with my value. Some things my family provided for me didn't align with me or no longer served me and others did align and continue to serve me.

Marriage and Divorce

An example, my family pattern is to get married, have children and remain married. Divorce was not an option. This expectation was hardwired into me, not only from my family, but it was also clearly echoed in my box of religion. Although my family upheld these expectations, I observed family members on both my paternal and maternal sides (and within the church) who were miserable in their marriages, and some of them were unhealthy marriages.

I recall attending a wedding anniversary celebration for a couple and the wife, thinking she was speaking quietly, commented, “I don’t know why everyone is so happy; I am not happy.” She then put on a mask and continued smiling throughout the event.

I love and honor the institution of marriage. At the same time, I am adamant that I will not remain in an unhealthy or toxic marriage or relationship. As I dated, I was in and out of relationships because once I saw the handwriting on the wall, I kept it moving. With this, I found myself married three times. Why? Because I refused to remain in any unhealthy relationships.

I tell you, I received backlash from my decisions. In two of my marriages, I was told, “You have to stay,” but I thought, “Hogwash, no, I don’t! This is not working.” Was there a battle in my mind about leaving? Yes, because I was torn between deciding for myself and “doing the right thing.” Did I feel like I failed because I didn’t live up to the “status quo” and remained married? Yes, absolutely. Divorce was an option for me (and for later generations), but it was not an option from my family box and religion box. I had to learn that critical thinking for myself is okay. And it’s okay for you also.

Because my family and religion box expected differently, did I feel ashamed of divorcing? Yes, I felt shamed by family members and others in the church. But I needed to decide for myself what was best and healthy for me, not what was best and healthy for my family nor church.

And it’s true, the third time is a charm; my knight in shining armor finally found me, and my current marriage is fabulous.

What does this mean to you?

Doing things "the right way" sometimes does not align with your historical and generational expectations of others. I am not saying that anyone needs to remain in their relationship. Nor am I saying that anyone should leave their relationship. What I'm saying is you need to make decisions for yourself and honor their values. Sidenote: It is never okay for people to be subjected to domestic violence, please seek help.

Making Decisions

What decisions have you made to try to uphold historical and generational patterns, traditions, and expectations from your family box?

What will happen if you continue to make decisions that don't align with you or no longer serve you?

How would things look different in your life as you apply the emotional CPR.ed process?

The family box drives us to make decisions. As I attempted to carry on and live out historical and generational patterns, traditions, and expectations of others, the ups and downs, and the ins and outs of my earlier life, were rough as I continued to attempt to "do the right thing." When it wasn't "the right thing," I made a mess of things even more as I attempted to "fix" the mess. Whew, it was a vicious cycle.

As I teach and coach others, I see them grappling with the ups and downs, the ins and outs, as they try to meet the historical and generational expectations of others. It's crucial to stop losing pieces of yourself in the pursuit of pleasing people. People-pleasing can lead to panic attacks, headaches, stomach aches, depression, mental health concerns, and alarmingly, I have known people to experience suicidal ideations or even commit suicide. Why do these outcomes occur? It's often because people try to be someone they aren't. Eventually, the strain of pretending or disappointing others becomes too much and takes a toll on all aspects of your life.

But there is good news! You don't have to go through the same ordeal. Take control of your life, identify your own values, and make decisions for yourself. You might not always get it right, and that's okay. Learn from your experiences, course-correct, and keep moving forward, upward, and onward. Hit the reset button and start living your own life, not someone else's.

At one point in my life, I thought I had it all together. However, as I continued living and experiencing life, it felt as if I was unraveling. I had to examine my thought process, along with the why and how I made decisions. Now hear me clearly, although it is important and necessary to seek guidance, and bounce ideas off someone, at the end of the day, you must make your own decision.

Are my thoughts, feelings, behaviors, and decisions truly my own? Are your thoughts, feelings, behaviors, and decisions truly your own or are they influenced by my family box? Or by other external factors?

What's your decision-making process?

I had to look again in the mirror and ask myself the $10 trillion dollar question, "Who am I?" "What do I believe?" "What do I want?"

I began to have clarity as I dealt with the reality that there were discrepancies between my perspectives and opinions and that of my family. Living up to my family box was hard was hard at times. The expectations were pressing me flat, like the big truck rolling over hot gravel to make the street level.

Take a stab at it, and answer the $10 trillion dollar, "Who are you?"

As you explore your identity, the process is not easy all the time. However, it will be rewarding. Applying the emotional CPR.ed process brings results in freedom as you glean clarity, understand purpose, and deal with some harsh realities. Yes, the process may be emotional, and remember, emotions are normal, and it's okay to own your feelings. Despite what your family box says, you are human, and emotions are human. Managing your emotions is needed, you make wise and sound decisions opposed to emotional decisions.

If you think embracing your emotions as you walk your discovery journey is daunting, imagine the continued impact of discontentment and chaos that's created when you don't manage your emotions. No more living the same year, year after year. I had to shift and decide I wanted to do something different as I continued to connect with "who I am."

What's on your mind?

Being You Outside of Your Family

For a long time, I wasn't just Karen; instead, I was known as a "Williams," a "Jones," and then known as my siblings to the tune of, "little Ella," "little Jack," "little Mike," or "little Ronda." Now, don't get me wrong, my siblings are fantastic and AWESOME! My Williams and Jones families are the best! I wouldn't trade either side of my family for anything. I love them all, and we are AMAZING! And, even amidst this AMAZINGNESS, I wanted to be my own kind of amazing, to just be Karen. Remember, although your family is cut from the same cloth, you are still an individual. As you move forward, your values may change, and that's perfectly okay!

I evolved from being defined as a "Williams," a "Jones," or "someone's little sister," to being defined as a "wife," "Faythe's mom," or "Kaleb's mom," and then, as a "Tyler," and a "bonus mom." But the titles didn't stop there. As I journeyed through life, I then was defined as a "boss," a "leader," a "professor," and now a "life coach." These are titles; they are not who I am. I have heard and observed others experiencing the same.

And you, my friend, are more than your family title or roles (we'll delve into the box of roles soon). When your family titles and roles are stripped away, you are left to examine, "Who am I?" Unpacking the question of who you are takes time because your identity is hardwired by historical and generational traditions, patterns and expectations of others.

In addition to family, faith is another value of mine. Self-love, independence, caring for others, serving, working hard, and giving back are other family values I embrace. I am grateful and appreciative of my parents, my nuclear family, and both sides of my extended family, who laid a foundation for me with values that I still hold close, like a cherished teddy bear.

What are some of your family values?

How do your family values align or don't align with your personal values?

Expectations of Cleanliness

Cleanliness is another family value I embrace. What has shifted is the pathway to how to clean. Cleaning was a huge undertaking as I grew up. First thing Saturday mornings, the expectation was we cleaned before we turned on the television. As I became a parent, I attempted to continue the same pattern, and this was not realistic. Times were different, and Saturday mornings was a need to sleep in after a long week of work, school, extracurricular activities and other commitments. Spring Break was named Clean Up Week, and that's what we did, we cleaned. Spring Break was not a break; we did not travel, nor did we go on vacation. Vacationing was visiting our family in Mississippi or Michigan during the summer.

Clean Up Week involved taking curtains down, washing them, ironing them, and rehanging them. Furniture was moved around as we mopped and vacuumed. Baseboards were cleaned, and dusting was taking place everywhere. Cleaning water that included soap, pine-sol, and bleach was boiled on the stove. We washed walls, doors, windows and figurines. Again, there is nothing wrong with this way of cleaning. It's not right, nor wrong, it's just different. The concern comes when this way of cleaning is no longer a choice, and instead, it becomes an expectation.

I still value cleanliness. After becoming a wife, a working mom, and a school mom, I did not have the time to "clean" the same way. I struggled for a long time, trying to keep up with the same patterns and expectations of cleaning that I grew up with. Furthermore, I have driven my children and husband up the wall about defining what constitutes cleanliness. Especially when my expectations are to clean, to the tune of "mommy clean."

Not only did I stress my children and husband out, but I also stressed myself out while attempting to maintain family patterns and expectations. I struggled for a long time, thinking of hiring a cleaning service to clean my home. Why? Because other women in my family did it all, they were superwomen and wonder women, so I thought.

But, as I applied the emotional CPR.ed process, I gained clarity that the women weren't doing the cleaning. They had lots of children who were keeping the house clean. My reality was I only had two children at home. And when they were younger, the responsibility to clean fell on my shoulders. As my children grew older and attended school, they participated in a lot of activities, and they didn't have time to clean up that way while using the same approach (I didn't either).

Why did I clean like that? Because "that's just the way we do it" or "because I said so," and this was not only in my household. This was the same expectation when visiting other family members.

Now, hear me out as I share from a kind, gentle and tender heart. Responses like "That's just the way we do it" and "because I said so," do not provide clarity or an understanding of purpose. It's not emotionally, physically, and/or mentally unhealthy to continue embracing unexplainable and nonproductive expectations. You must confront your realities of historical and generational patterns and expectations set by others.

With this realization, I decided to hire a cleaning service to clean my home thoroughly. This was one of the best decisions of my life. My stress level decreased, and I had more time to do other things that needed to be done, and to spend more time with my family.

And yes, family members had opinions about my decision. I had to listen to comments like, "Girl, why did you get a cleaning service?" "You're wasting money," "You know you can clean yourself," and "Honey, give me that money, I'll clean your house." These conversations went in one ear and out the other. I had to let people feel and say what they wanted. I started living my life while managing my emotions and stopped people-pleasing as I made decisions.

At the end of the day, as I adapt, reset and shift to a growth mind-set, I get to decide how and if historical and generational patterns and expectations still serve me. The Clean Up Week approach no longer served me. I decided we'd travel throughout the United States and to other countries during Spring Break. For alignment in my life, there was a need to decide what works for me and my nuclear family and to finally stop trying to be Superwoman and Wonder Woman and just be Karen.

What do you need to be mindful of as you make decisions for you opposed to for your family?

Viewing Things from Different Perspectives

1. Listening to stories and observing how my family grew up having very little, working long hours as they picked cotton, and encountering racism has taught me many spoken and unspoken lessons. One lesson I have learned is that people can't tell you what you can and can't do, that is the way of slavery, the way of living in the South. You get to determine what you can and can't do. Don't allow other people to dictate your life and write your story.
2. The goal is to move forward and not be consumed by what happens to you. I suggest you look at things from a different perspective. Take control of how you navigate through what happens to you as you apply the CPR.ed framework and look at both sides of the coin. You have control over some things you experience and others you don't. At the same time, things that happened in your family or things you learned from your family box, at times will require you to shift as you live your life.

As it was with my children, although some chapters of their story were written for them, that's not who they are. The same can be true for you, in that although some chapters of your story are written for you, that's not who you are. Things may have happened to you, that's not who you are. Take the pen, write future chapters, and define who you are. Do not give power, control, or permission to people or your family box. You are responsible for making decisions that align with your values.

Let's pause, reflect on your family. What's coming up for you as you explore both sides of your family's coin?

3. Behaviors and patterns are learned not only from environment, but also by personality because of DNS. The reality some of you may encounter is you don't own or acknowledge your paternal and maternal family. This does not change the fact that they are still your family, and they have a role in how you are shaped. The reality for some of you is you may be disowned, rejected, not acknowledged or accepted by your family. That's horrible, and I apologize to you for having to experience this. In either case, as you explore your identity, shift to a growth mindset and shift your perspective, learn how to manage through your emotions as a result to either of the above. When you do so, you are able to make sound and wise decisions to align with your values.

   As you explore dark, hard, hurtful, disappointing, and unacceptable situations, how can you allow your experience to help you to grow, shift, or propel you forward to thriving and freedom? In doing so, you get to view things from different perspectives in search of fun times and good times to cling to.

As an adult, while applying emotional CPR.ed to my family box, I had to release some of the anger I felt towards my parents for being "strict and rigid." Looking at situations from different perspectives, I understood that their "strict and rigid" approach and numerous answers of "No" were meant to keep me safe. Their purpose and intent weren't to confine or limit me but to prepare me for life. While understanding that as this was happening, my identity was shaped to be "strict and rigid," but that's not who I am. I have decided to shift to a growth mindset and decide to embrace the open, warm, curious, and free person that I truly am.

Let's pause for a moment. Despite the REALLY challenging, hard, unforgivable, and rocky experiences you may have experienced within your that has shaped you, where do you need to see things from both sides of the coin, from various perspectives and shift to be true to yourself?

What areas of your life do you need to take ownership and responsibility to heal in pursuit of managing through emotions that will support you to make wise decisions?

Is my family perfect? No. Is your family perfect? No.

Peeking into my box of family has been a journey to discover who I am. There were and still are many layers to peel back as I seek to find Karen through it all. Yes, I appreciate the chapters written for me, but now I must take ownership and responsibility for my own life to write my next chapters, defining who I am. I may not be responsible for what may have happened, or what has been my experience, and at the same time, again, it's my responsibility to heal where needed. And it's the same for you; you can do the same. When we do, we are in a better position to align our life accordingly as we grow into who we really are.

What does it look like for you to peek into your family box as you explore who you really are?

What's one step you will take to begin to be your authentic and true self?

Oh, my goodness, this is SO exciting, my friend. You get to be released from group think. You get to be set free from being imprisoned by historical and generational traditions, patterns and expectations of others. You get to be delivered from thoughts, feelings, and behaviors of others that don't belong to you and set boundaries in pursuit of embracing yourself.

No more obligation! No more guilt!

Guess what's next— the box of roles. Come on, let's dive in as you explore, undo who you have become and get out of the box to hit the button, Identity ReSet 4: Roles: Not Me!

Turn the page.

Identity ReSet 4: Roles (or Gender):

NOT ME!

Roles: Not Me!

Think Through It

Roles appear in various forms, such as your occupation, a leader, student, employee, parent, child (sibling position), spouse, caregiver, friend, etc. Although there are many types of roles (positions or titles), we'll explore two roles that impact the formation of your identity: gender and family positioning.

What other roles come to mind?

Gender roles come with said expectations of what males and females "should do" and "shouldn't do." How males and females "should act" and "shouldn't act." Or what's "acceptable" and "what's not acceptable" for males and females. These 'said' expectations play a major role in shaping our identities.

Your family positioning of being the oldest child, middle child, or youngest child carries "weight," "stigmas," or "myths" while dictating expectations of others. The role as a dad, mom, grandparent, stepparent, and even father/mother, sister/brother-in-law are enmeshed with "said expectations" of who you are, "what you should do," or "how you should act." And before you know it, because it's the "said way," you attempt to live up to those expectations while, at the same time, finding yourself trapped in the box of roles.

Being a leader also comes with "said" expectations of how you should behave. Attempting to fit the mold of being a leader leaves you scrambling to fill the expectations of that role. One of the greatest myths of a leader is that leaders have ALL the answers. Come on now! Can one person possibly have ALL the answers? Absolutely not! But, somehow, leaders having ALL the answers continue to be an expectation that people attempt to uphold and eventually lose sight of who they are during the process.

What other myths come to mind about the expectations of being a leader?

Expectations of roles force you into a box and interrupt your ability to truly be yourself. Trying to fit a mold, in turn, forces you to pretend as you paste on your mask in pursuit of adapting to the historical and generational patterns, traditions, and expectations of others. Unfortunately, you lose yourself slowly, day by day, and year by year.

What happens when you strive to meet unrealistic expectations and conform to the "status quo" of roles? You guessed it; you can become overwhelmed, stressed, depressed, or even experience physical ailments.

Let's reflect on my awakening experience as I volunteered during my class. It was at that moment I began to realize I was trapped in the box of roles, like a clown stuffed into a jack-in-the-box. I was suffocating while trying to fulfill the roles of being a female, a wife, a mom, and a leader. I later became aware of how being the youngest child in my family impacted me in ways that clashed with my beliefs, perspectives, and values.

What patterns, traditions, and expectations are in your box of roles?

Where did they originate?

Who started these expectations?

Mine stem from my deep Southern family roots, television shows, societal expectations, and my box of family, culture and religion. Trying to live up to these expectations requires A LOT of work.

My experience has been that females are expected to belong in the kitchen and maintain a clean house, while males work outside of the house, take out the trash, and maintain the exterior upkeep of the home (i.e., mowing or maintaining the lawn/landscape, shoveling snow, etc.).

Expectations says, "That's just the way it is," "that's what I am supposed to do," "how I am supposed to act," and that's "what's expected of me," as a female.

These limiting messages left me in shambles at times to comply, and other times, I negated them because I really didn't embrace nor believe in these expectations. Behaving any differently than what's expected placed me in a corner, with a cone on my head, and earned me a new identifier, a new title, a new role, to the tune of being "a pot stirrer, defiant, a rebel," or "one to go against the grain." But I am not any of these identifiers; I just hold different perspectives, opinions, and values as it relates to expectations of females and males.

It is okay for you to own your opinion, perspective, and values while allowing others the liberty to do the same. Living up to the said expectations is neither right nor wrong; it's just different. Either work and identifying with one or not identifying with one should be a choice and not an expectation.

The danger arises when other people's opinions, perspectives, and values are forced upon or expected of you. You then lose sight of who you are when you attempt to own and live out someone else's experience or decision and adapt to their way of living as your own. Remember, doing so may lead to anxiety, depression, mental health, and medical concerns. And as you stand in truth, you will experience freedom as you honor and make decisions that align with your values.

What are the limiting messages you experienced about the roles of females and males?

Stay Home Parent

My mother, paternal and maternal grandmothers, and my maternal great-grandmothers were all housewives. I still have aunts, cousins, and other relatives who are homemakers, housewives, or stay-at-home moms. With this, my mindset was shaped so that when I began to have babies, I was to stay at home with my children.

Let's begin with acknowledging that there is absolutely NOTHING wrong with being a housewife, homemaker, or stay-at-home mom. The concern arises when it is "expected" that females should exclusively live out these roles. Women should have the liberty to make their own decisions and should not feel forced or pressured to fulfill these roles based on the patterns, traditions, and expectations of others. Your identity becomes compromised when, one, these roles become who you are and, two, you feel like you "have to" live out these roles.

I've encountered men who, unfortunately, were ostracized, judged, and criticized because they chose to stay home to care for their children. This is highly unfortunate! It's perfectly okay for both men and women to make decisions that best fit their household. These decisions should not be dictated by historical, generational, nor societal or cultural expectations and norms.

What will you do differently to avoid judging someone else when your decision differs from theirs?

Let's pause for a moment and apply the emotional CPR.ed process to the discussion of who should stay at home with the children. For clarity, it's essential to understand the family's needs. The purpose or goal is for someone to be at home, caring for the children. The reality is that it doesn't matter whether it's the dad or the mom. Yes, this reality may cause discomfort, especially when it contradicts what you know, what you've been taught or what you've learned and what you know.

Yes, emotions will surface as you grapple with criticisms and listen to others being judgmental or not accepting you as a person, nor respecting your decision. The goal is to manage your emotions, allowing other people to own their thoughts, opinions, and values. As you manage your emotions, you will then be able to make sound decisions (as opposed to emotional and reactionary decisions) that honor you, your values and your family.

How will the emotional CPR.ed process support you as you explore your own box of roles?

I was a stay-at-home mom twice to uphold deeply driven expectations of the role of a mom. I absolutely enjoyed being home with my children. When they began attending school, there was joy in dropping them before and after school every day. Being a hot lunch mom, classroom mom, prayer mom, and an all-around person let me know what you need mom to support my children, their school, and administration was priceless. And at the same time, I felt as if something was missing.

It was thrilling to share a snack or go to the park with my children. I enjoyed spending the evening with them and having dinner prepared when my husband arrived home. And I tell you; it is indescribable not to have the stress of the competing need to do laundry, go grocery shopping, and to clean while balancing the expectations and demands of working outside of the home, driving or riding back and forth to work, etc.

At the same time, I was conflicted and battling internally, as I yearned for more than just caring for my children and tending to my home. I also enjoyed working outside of my home. I needed to get out and connect with others beyond my school community. There was a financial sacrifice that came with staying home and not earning a paycheck. However, finances NEVER compare to the benefits of being home with my children. Money CANNOT replace the bonds, memories, and relationships formed with my children.

Why do families have to make such a difficult choice?

Parents need to pause and deal with realities as they make decisions for themselves, not based on historical and generational patterns, traditions, and expectations of others. One reality to consider is the financial sacrifice of being a stay-at-home parent. Then there's the fact that sometimes working outside the house doesn't necessarily translate to additional income in the household. After accounting for childcare expenses, before and after care and/or transportation, gas for the car, monthly train/bus tickets, clothing costs, cleaning bills for those clothes, funds for lunch, snacks, etc., you find you're working mainly to cover these expenses. Ultimately, the decision belongs to each person and conforming to expectations can shift your identity.

Again, staying home with your children is neither right nor wrong. It's a decision that both moms and dads must make. Families have the liberty to decide for the dad to remain home, and this doesn't make him any less of a man. These decisions should not be based on the boxes of roles. Let's not judge anyone based on our experiences, expectations, or values. We should allow people to be who they are and honor decisions they make for their family.

As a little girl, I observed the role of dads to be financially responsible for the home, while moms were responsible for caring for the home and children. This was prevalent with my paternal and maternal sides of my family. Later, it became confusing, as I noticed a shift with moms working outside the home. At the same time, there were women in my family and community who stayed home to care for the children.

Talk about a child in conflict growing up. I could not figure out who decided when a female would stay at home and when she should work outside of the home. And it was further confusing because who changed the rules? My point exactly: rules and expectations are based on someone else's experience and decisions.

Also, with roles, I observed my dad and uncles stand over a grill and barbecue while my mom and aunts prepared the side meals in the kitchen. Whew, I tell you, the smell of the meat, spaghetti, baked beans, and potato salad left me salivating in anticipation of the final meal.

Many times, my role as a girl was that of what I call "a runner." As the females prepped the meat in the kitchen, I took it outside to the males at the grill. When the males were done cooking the meat, I then took the meat back to the kitchen to the females.

Then, it was the role of the males to make their famous barbecue sauce from scratch. As the males were preparing the barbecue sauce, the desserts (cakes, pies, banana pudding, homemade ice cream, peach cobbler, etc.) were being prepared by, guess by who? You got it, the females. But I have a cousin and other male family members who broke that mold of roles. He makes the best caramel cake and other male family members cook full meals, and they are delicious. They got out of that box of roles, and you can, too.

What are the expectations of roles in your family? What do YOU believe about those expectations?

I vividly remember attending family gatherings in the South in Mississippi and up North in Chicago, where the males would sit together, laughing, watching television, talking, and enjoying each other's company. And the females? You guessed it, they were in the kitchen.

When it was time to eat, everyone gathered, said grace, and gave thanks. The males would then return to their gathering room, waiting patiently for the females to prepare their meals and deliver their plates. This involved a lot of zipping back-and-forth trips to the kitchen as the males made various requests, and the females worked diligently to fulfilling them.

But it didn't end there. After the males finished eating, the roller skate disco dance routine would start all over again. The females would collect the males' dinner plates and then serve them dessert. There were even times when the males would enter the kitchen, make a specific request, and specify how much or how little of a particular food item they wanted.

The males would then return to the room with their male peers, followed by the females carrying their plates. The females would hand over the plates to the males once they were seated. This expectation observed during family gatherings highlighted the distinct roles and expectations within my family.

Now there is absolutely NOTHING wrong with individuals deciding how they live out roles and responsibilities. The challenge, however, arises when the roles and responsibilities become rigid expectations that define who you are. The challenge is that when you don't have a choice, because of expectations. It becomes even more concerning, when people really don't believe in certain expectations, but continue to live up to them "save face," or to avoid embarrassment because you are not keeping up with "the norm."

When patterns, traditions, and the expectations of others dictate your identity, you risk losing yourself. To be clear, again, I am not saying the roles and responsibilities of anyone's experience are inherently the "right" way or the "wrong" way; they are simply just different. Each person has the right to decide what they believe, value, and how they live their life.

What are your thoughts?

My expectations of roles differed from what I was taught and observed, and that's perfectly okay, well for me at least. I used to wonder, "What's wrong with the males? I see their feet and hands working, but why don't they prepare their own meals? Can't they get up and empty their plates like everyone else?"

When I asked these questions, I never received an answer; instead, I was often told to "be quiet, go sit down." Or, on a good day, I would receive a stern stare, which clearly meant, "Shut your mouth and take the plate to the male."

I was all too familiar with those phrases, facial expressions and the expectation to be quiet and not say a word. There I was, muzzled and muted. I would think, "Oh my, here we go again." I was curious and just needed the logic to make sense. In my family, the roles and expectations of females were strict, clearly defined and crystal clear. Although I didn't agree with these expectations and didn't think they were fair, over time, the box of roles became my norm.

What has become your norm?

My Norm Came Crashing Down

My norm came crashing down after I married. My husband experienced different historical and generational patterns, traditions, and expectations of roles. Although he was born in Mississippi, he was not entrenched in the Southern expectations of roles and responsibilities of the south as it relates to roles.

My husband not only provides for our home; he also cleans and loves cooking and grocery shopping. I was a bit taken aback as I asked myself,

"Who is this man," and "Where did he come from?" I had to gain clarity that the world was not governed by my "norm" nor by my historical and generational patterns, traditions, and expectations of others. What an awakening!

On one hand, I thought, "Look here, I hit the jackpot!" On the other hand, there was work to be done in our marriage because we each had different experiences and expectations of roles. We had to work together to determine what worked best for us and for our marriage. Not what he or I was familiar with, nor what he or I was accustomed to, and not what the box of roles dictated, but what worked for us.

As I made decisions for myself, outside of my family pattern, traditions, and expectations, marriage began to look different for me. Again, difference doesn't mean one way is right and the other way is wrong. It's just different. It was okay for me to shift because I never, deep down within, accepted nor embraced the functioning of roles and responsibilities in my box.

Standing in my truth was a journey, and although I hated the historical and generational expectations and despised stereotypes, I still wrestled with my deep-rooted Southern experiences. My identity was wrapped up and tangled up with ideas that had been drilled into me about the roles and responsibilities of males and females. I found myself at a crossroads and had to explore the hard questions. "What do I really believe?" "What works for me? I had to begin to fight my way out of the box of roles and be prepared for others not to be okay with my decisions.

After much reflection and MANY conversations with myself as I wrestled with my two worlds, I gained clarity that I didn't truly believe the expectation that females should prepare dinner plates for males, even though I felt compelled to uphold this way of thinking and living.

This transition was an emotional roller coaster as I faced my reality. It enabled me to make decisions to stand in my truth, to be authentic and live life for myself. My anxiety stemmed more from what my family would think and my reluctance to deal with potential "harassment" about my decision. I didn't want to be bullied or pressured into living my life aligned with the box of roles.

But I walked boldly in courage, no longer feeling guilty about sitting down while my husband cooked, prepared his plate (and mine too, which was SO cool), and cleaned up. I began to be comfortable with him going grocery shopping. My friend, I had arrived at a place of freedom I needed to protect and maintain, as some of my paternal and maternal family members viewed and lived out their lives differently regarding roles. My new approach to roles was going well in my marriage until we visited my parents' home and other family members' homes and attended larger family gatherings.

During these times, it was as if the box of roles tried to overpower and overtake me, like being in a fight after school on the playground. I struggled because my parents and other people struggled with the expectations of roles in my marriage. My truth clashed violently with their deep-rooted expectations of the roles and responsibilities of males and females. I had to manage my emotions when confronted with comments like, "You know you are supposed to fix his plate," or "How can you eat before your husband has?" This happened not only at my parents' home but also in other family settings.

After many rounds of this rodeo show, I had to pause, hold my parents' hands as we stood face to face, and share how expectations of roles existed in my marriage. I also shared that I respected their experience and their expectations in their marriage and requested they respect mine. It wasn't until then that we agreed to disagree, as they slowly accepted my reality that the roles of males and females danced to a different tune and beat in my marriage.

I must pause for a moment and ask: Who linked the responsibilities of roles with expectations of basic life skills that everyone needs, males and females? Both males and females should know how to cook, clean, budget and pay bills, drive, and take care of children. Somehow, these basic life skills became segregated into roles designated exclusively for males and females.

I find myself still honoring my family's historical and generational patterns, traditions, and expectations: to get married, work together, and take care of each other, the home, and the children. However, carrying out these actions looks different to me. And remember, as we say, "Different is not about one being right and the other wrong; it's just different."

What does it look like to thrive in life and be free from expectations of the box of roles?

So, I thought I was out of the woods. I had removed the mask and began living in freedom, free from the bond of my box of roles. I was honoring my decision and my marriage until we attended a large family gathering with my extended family. We gathered around the table for dinner, said grace, and then a line formed to prepare meals. I prepared my plate, plates for my children, and sat down to eat. This was the norm in my house after marriage. But as I was eating, I was abruptly disturbed by a family member who was livid that I didn't prepare my husband's plate. This person approached me, and the conversation went like this:

Family Member (yelling with a nasty tone): "How dare you fix your own plate, sit down to eat, and your husband hasn't eaten yet?

Me (very politely, because I was no longer a prisoner in the box of roles):

He's good; he likes to prepare his own plate."

Oh my, Geesh, and what did I say that for? The conversation went south fast, just as it did after I responded to my uncle during my conversation about me not being able to go to the "white mall."

Family Member (came at me like a mad fighter in a ring): What are you talking about?

Me: Blank stare as I digress.

Then, another family member jumped into the conversation and joined in with the bullying, as they DEMANDED that I prepare my husband's plate. Because, of course, "That's what I'm supposed to do." The two of them were in my face as I attempted to explain the expectation of the role of my husband in our marriage was his request to prepare his own plate.

Then my hunk of a husband humbly walked over to save his beauty, to rescue his damsel in distress— me. He calmly said to them, "It's okay;

Karen can eat. I can prepare my own plate. She doesn't make my plate; I like to fix my own plate, and she can finish eating."

And, of course, that did not go over well at all. Both of my family members double-teamed my husband, attempting to "set him" straight. They cornered him, with one of them stating, "What do you mean, Karen is not to prepare your plate? She CANNOT sit down and eat, and you haven't eaten." Really, how do you tell a grown man who has decided, that the expectation in his marriage is incorrect?

They went on and on while my sweet husband tried to reason with them. He was confused about what the big deal was about and appalled by their reaction. He continued to engage in an open-minded conversation with people who were clearly closed-minded and had super-fixed mindsets. There was nothing wrong with his view, nor was there anything wrong with their views. Their views and expectations were simply different.

How do you handle situations when your values and expectations differ from others?

Unfortunately, I was overwhelmed by my bundle of emotions. Sadly, I retreated from being bold and courageous, and standing in my truth. I compromised what I believed, while putting my mask back on, shrinking back, and allowing my emotions to drive my decisions, as I jumped back into the box of roles. I waved my white flag as I sat in the box of roles, surrendering my freedom. I felt trapped and jailed.

I stood off at a distance as I left my poor husband to hang out to dry and fend for himself. I began to second guess myself as on one hand, I welcomed and allowed my family to thrust me back into the box of roles, and on the other hand, I jumped back into the box myself.

I did not condone nor support my family's expectations of roles and responsibilities of females and males, and at that moment, I did not allow myself to be me. I did not open my mouth to speak up on my husband's behalf, nor honored and respected my marriage.

Instead, I was vigorously shaking my head "no" to him in disagreement as I waved my hands uncontrollably, like a drowning person in a sea of water, begging for the drowning to end. I was trying to get him to do what I resented hearing all my life: the very thing that has kept me muzzled, silent, and in a box. I just needed him to "be quiet". Many emotions flooded my warm and nervous body as I thought, "Just stop! Give up, dude; this is one you will not win.

My husband just did not get it. I wondered, "What is wrong with him?" Nothing was wrong with him. My family was attempting to control him and force him to become someone who he wasn't. They wanted him to comply with what they knew, with what they were familiar and comfortable with. They wanted both of us to comply with the box of roles. I thought, "Okay, this is my third marriage, I have got to get this one right."

But, at that moment, I was arrested by the limited message of "be silent." I allowed myself to be entangled again with "That's the way it has always been" and "This is the way it is." I was giving up a piece of myself and not honoring myself, and this shook me to my core.

At the same time, while I hated the patterns, traditions, and expectations of roles, I was SO pressed back into the box of roles and overcome by the emotions that flooded my mind, soul, and body that I automatically returned to pleasing my family, to, "keep the peace." In my box of religion, some will say, my response was a sign of humility. But humility is about setting boundaries and speaking (not arguing) your truth. What I did was dishonor myself, my husband, and my marriage. Sadly, I caved in.

What situation have you faced where you surrendered a piece of yourself in the process of trying to please others?

Wow! I hated it! How did I fall back into this box of roles?

How do I return to standing firm in what I believe, standing in

my truth?

How can I consistently be myself and live my life?

Well, what does this mean for you (and for me)?

It means that today is a new day, and tomorrow is coming. When you encounter challenges like I did, apply the emotional CPR.ed process, which is what I should have done. Hit the reset button as you manage your emotions to support living your life and making decisions for yourself. The CPR.ed process isn't a one-time solution. It's a continuous process, a way of being that you must consistently practice.

Just as I learned, and as I teach and coach others, you must persistently dig and work at it. Give yourself grace when you regress, like I did. Forgive yourself, decide to continue being you, and stay out of the box of roles. Initially, it may not be comfortable, but the more you apply the emotional CPR.ed process, the more freedom you will experience. I know this to be true as I've moved upward, forward, and onward, despite my hiccups.

Will fear be present? Yes.

Are there risks? Yes.

Will relationships shift and change? Yes.

As you manage through your emotions, will there be freedom as you make wise decisions? Absolutely, yes!

All these questions lead you to confront your realities. While the process may be uncomfortable at times, it's even harder to remain the same, to people-please, and live in a box.

What does it look like to live your life outside of the box of roles?

Remaining in the role box is no longer an option for you. There's so much more outside of the box! Life, like a roller coaster, has ups and downs, dips, and unexpected turns, so will you. As you transition, be mindful of how historical and generational patterns, traditions, and expectations either exist or don't exist in your life.

Take a moment; I welcome you to look out over the mountain. What does it look like for you to make your own decisions about roles and responsibilities of males and females?

Family Positioning:

Being the youngest child of five, I often didn't have a voice and felt as if I was smothered. There were times when I felt unseen, unimportant, and that my thoughts and opinions were not taken seriously, welcomed, or valued. Because I was the last child, I spent a lot of time aggressively inserting myself while fighting to have my voice heard and my presence acknowledged. Even today, there are times that I digress when I feel that I am not heard, seen, included, or as if I don't have an opinion, or what I have to say doesn't matter. Being aggressive is who I have become at times.

Who is Karen? I am a unique person. I am kind, curious, funny, witty, creative, see things differently, and I am a giver. I love myself, and at times, I feel like I don't fit in because I think differently and dance to a different beat. My beat and tune are different from that of my historical and generational expectations.

Here's how situations worked in my family in relation to the "rank" of sibling positioning. My oldest sister and oldest brother assisted my parents with caring for the house and younger children. I recall situations where my dad requested my oldest sister to complete a task. She then told my oldest brother to get it done, and he, in turn, instructed my other brother to complete the task.

You see where I'm going with this, right?

That brother instructed my other sister to complete the task, and of course, she passed the torch to me. At that point, the buck stopped with me, the youngest child; I had no one to boss around. Despite how I felt or what I thought, I was left with no voice and without a choice, as I silently but angrily complied.

I constantly found myself needing to fight for myself and find my identity. I have a name, and I am a whole person. Remember, I was referred to as "the little sister" to my siblings or as "a Williams" or "a Jones." I just wanted to be me, Karen.

My daughter looks like me (acts like me, too), and we have a lot in common. Despite the similarities, and in efforts for her to own her identity,

I have always told her, "You may look like me and act alike, but you are not me; be your own person."

Because of my childhood experience, I constantly remind my son and my daughter to be unique, to be you. For them to be leaders, not a follower, as they function as the thermostat and regulate the temperature in a room. My heart's desire is for my children to have clarity about who they are, stand in truth, and make decisions for themselves, even in the face of historical and generational patterns, traditions, and expectations. I need them to be their own person, although they are connected to our family.

Being identified as the youngest sibling, and according to my family surname, happens often. It was very prevalent at school, with the students, teachers, and administration. One time, I had a fight at school and had to stand outside of my classroom. As the administrator was on her way to my classroom, she turned the corner to find me standing there. She then shook her head and said, "Oh no, not a Williams, this can't be."

Just when I thought I had cleared a new path for myself while transitioning to Chicago Vocational High School (CVS), it all started again. You see, my oldest sister attended the same school 12 years prior. So, I thought I would have my own space, free to be myself. However, once the teachers realized I was her younger sister, the overshadow of being someone else's little sister began again. I felt like I constantly had to remind people, "Hello, I'm here," "It's me, Karen, remember me?"

Now, there's absolutely nothing wrong with being a sister to my siblings; they are the bomb! They are awesome and cool. There's no issue with me being a "Williams," nor being a "Jones." I am proud to be connected to my family. As I shared earlier, despite disagreements, challenges, and differences, my family's foundation equipped me well for adulthood. I am honored and grateful to be part of my family.

WAKE UP!

There are myths about family roles. For instance, the oldest child is often labeled as the most responsible, the middle child as sensitive, the youngest child as spoiled, and the only child as selfish. There are also myths that in-laws are controlling, custodial parents are strict, and non-custodial parents are fun parents.

All these expectations are subjective, generalizations and stereotypes. Yet, for some reason, people adopt, adapt and assimilate to said expectations as routinely as people get dressed every day. Daily people continue to put on clothes that don't fit, just as people attempt to live up to roles while conforming to historical and generational patterns, traditions and expectations of others.

What's your position in your family?

What expectations come along with your position?

There is nothing wrong with historical and generational expectations. The name of the game is to make decisions for yourself, to be you, because that's who you are, as opposed to becoming what your box of roles dictates.

It's important that you gain clarity about who you are, how you think, and what you believe. You get to decide how patterns, traditions, and expectations of others fit, or not, into your life. When you don't process situations and manage your emotions, you may tend to make decisions for the majority while continuing to perpetuate behaviors that show up later in your life.

An example of unprocessed feelings was seen as I showed up at work one day, feeling as if I was not heard. During a team meeting, we were discussing a matter. A question was asked, and the floor was open for discussion. As I was sharing my perspective and attempting to make my request, a co-worker abruptly halted the meeting, as his hands flew into the air, with a reply of, "Well, that's not going to happen; this is the way it is," and "I'm not changing it." Each time I attempted to engage him further in the conversation, he disrupted me and cut me off. My inner being immediately became defensive, guarded, and emotional.

That was it! My brain, along with my emotions, were hijacked, and my emotions took the lead, shooting off like a rocket headed to Mars. I felt completely invisible, as if I didn't have a voice. I was okay with being told "No." What I struggled with, and what bothered me, was feeling dismissed, feeling like my voice wasn't heard, as if I was not valued, and experienced feelings of being unimportant.

Just like that, in the blink of an eye, I experienced a flashback to my role in my family as the youngest sibling. You remember, the one who was always told what to do. Because I was emotionally charged, I reacted instead of responding. My behavior was ugly and unprofessional, and so was his.

But I am not responsible for him; I am only responsible for myself. Remember, who you are is not determined by how someone else responds or behaves. Who you are is determined by you, what you embrace and the decisions you make for yourself. You are in control of yourself, the roles you fill, and your life.

Later, my supervisor and I discussed the incident. I was asked, "Karen, what are you really upset about?" I was stuck, like a pole in cement, as I stumbled for an answer. As I paused and pondered why I was upset and applied the emotional CPR.ed process, I gained clarity, confronted reality head-on. I was hurt because I felt shut down, silenced, and muted. Those childhood feelings overflowed like a pot boiling over on the stove. I felt invisible as if my opinion didn't matter.

Remember, it's important for you to know who you are and be aware of how you show up each day. Your previous experiences shape how you show up. You must practice being attuned, as you show up as you and not as who you have become.

I'm sure you can see, my role as the youngest child in the family resurfaced later in life. The limiting messages from my childhood, which involved not being seen or heard, have significantly impacted who I have become. I invite you to pause, course-correct, and hit the reset button as you step out of the box of roles. This box can be paralyzing, leaving you struggling to be yourself.

While discussing historical, generational and expectations of others in this chapter on the box of roles, we haven't even touched on other stereotypes such as "males should not play with dolls or kitchen sets, nor express emotions" or "girls should wear pink, can't play with hot wheels cars, nor engage in male-dominated sports." Then there's the notion that females can't occupy certain positions or hold specific titles or roles in places of worship. And don't forget the outdated beliefs that females don't belong in the military, shouldn't work on construction sites, or that airline attendant positions are not suitable for males, and pilot positions are not suitable for females.

Unfortunately, these expectations of roles often define who we become. Whether or not the roles are embraced, remember, if they are, it should be decision. Your decision should not be deemed right or wrong simply because of patterns and expectations.

Who comes up with these expectations anyway?

These historical and generational patterns, traditions, and expectations continue to be passed down from generation to generation. There is nothing wrong with males or females participating in any of the activities previously mentioned. It's a choice and should not be an expectation, especially not someone else's expectation. Whatever decision you or someone else makes, it's yours or theirs. They may be different, and let's refrain from being judgmental. Instead, let's remember that one way is not right and the other wrong; they're just different.

What limiting messages about expectations of roles impact who you are today?

Where are you drowning, attempting to "fit" into the box of roles?

Trying to live up to expectations that you are not you, that you don't own, nor do they align with your truth and values, is exhausting as you wear a mask. What we know about masks is that they really don't cover up everything. And it's hard to breathe when you wear masks. Just stop, take off the mask, and be yourself.

WAKE UP!

The longer you continue to live up to society's expectations or your family's historical and generational patterns, traditions, and expectations of others, and don't honor your values, you will continue to struggle to be at peace. Don't allow another moment or day to pass that you lose a piece of yourself.

I invite you to hit the reset button, stop wearing your mask, and step out of the box of roles to experience freedom.

What would that look like to you?

What's one step you will take to wear your own shoes as you dance your way out of the box of roles?

No more wearing a mask! No more adapting or assimilating!

When you are done processing and exploring your box or roles, come on and go with me; let's keep digging as you read next about the box of religion, Identity ReSet 5: Religion: Why, Just Why?

Identity ReSet 5: Religion:

WHY? JUST WHY?

Religion: Why, Just Why?

Get Control of Your Life

Religion!

As you peer into your religion box, what do you see?

What do you really believe?

If you are not connected, nor have you been connected to any organized religion, what have you observed about religion?

In either case, your experience has driven you to make decisions or to not make decisions. For those of you who have not had a pleasant experience, been hurt by people, or hurt by a place of worship, I apologize to you for the unfortunate experience you have had.

Let's revisit the idea of your life as a book composed of many chapters, each holding experiences you've had. In any book, all chapters contribute to the overarching story of your life while building upon one another. You can't go back and re-write previous chapters of your book. But you can control the narrative of those chapters and begin to write your subsequent chapters. When you refrain from becoming the author of your own book and of your own life, by default, you choose to continue being defined and governed by your previous chapters, by your box of religion (or other boxes) and its practices that were written (or shoved down your throat) by someone else. However, when you seize the opportunity to take the pen in hand and start writing, you become the author of your own life story. The future chapters are your own and write. When you do this, you are no longer a victim, you begin to triumph over challenges and become victorious.

What does it look like for you to write your own story from this point forward?

You are strong! You are courageous! You are resilient! You matter! How exciting this is.

Now is the time for you to discover who you really are and not who you have become. It's your time to objectively explore what you truly believe as you shift to a growth mindset. You get to manage through your trauma, through your religious trauma that you may have experienced. In doing so, you experience mental health wellness and discontinue leaving a legacy of religious trauma to the next generation. You can apply the emotional CPR.ed process to support to define who you are and step out of the religion box to live a life of freedom.

A Strong Foundation

I am VERY appreciative and thankful for the strong spiritual foundation that was provided for me. This foundation has contributed to the knowledge and wisdom I have today. It has created a love for me to use my spiritual gifts to serve and help others, to teach, lead and support organizations while using the gift of administration. I will never trade my strong foundation for anything, despite some of the unfortunate experiences I have had while being strangled, choked and beat down by my box of religion.

My great-grandparents (and probably generations prior to them) laid a strong foundation for their children and future generations. Both my grandfathers and grandmothers were people of faith. My grandfather served as a deacon. My grandmother served in several capacities, and she could sing her heart out. I have great aunts and great uncles, aunts and uncles, and cousins who can make a room stand still while singing. For some reason, I COMPLETELY missed that boat when the gift to carry a note and sing was given out. Despite this, I still LOVE praise and worship.

Mom has served in many capacities in ministry also, and my dad also served. There are paternal and maternal family members in my family who are apostles, prophets, evangelists, pastors, and teachers. There are others who are ministers, preachers, deacons, ushers, missionaries, and administrators. Sidenote, remember, these are roles and titles they hold, and they don't define who they are. Keep in mind, your roles and titles don't define who you are.

Attending church is what I "learned" to do, and this has shaped who I have become, my view of myself and others and my view of the world. Going to church in Chicago up North or visiting the South in Mississippi, going to church is what we did. I attended church with my immediate family and with my extended family as well. I recall visiting two of my uncles, and I have fond memories of growing up with my cousins. We attended a lot of services and activities at their place of worship.

What's has been your experience?

While growing up, we went to church ALL the time. When I say ALL the time, I literally mean ALL the time. At times, it felt as if I spent more time at church than I did at home.

The week began on Sunday, with prayer, Sunday School Teacher preparation class and followed by Sunday School. Participating in a LONG service was next, followed by sitting in on Young People Willing Workers (YPWW) teachings. The day ended with the broadcast service and then a late-night service. Somewhere in between all the services, we would make our way back home to eat, stay at church or visit the storefront restaurant across the street from the church to grab a bite to eat.

Now, that was just Sunday. Monday through Saturday brought its own set of church-related activities. We would attend school, go home to eat, and then head straight to church. Somewhere, in between, homework and housework were still accomplished.

Monday through Friday consisted of bible study, youth group, Emmitt Till Player rehearsal, visiting the sick and shut-in for prayer, a mini service and to provide communion. Then there were other prayer services, shut ins, choir practice, occasional meetings, and Friday night service. As previously stated, I have a genuine love for praise and worship. And yes, although I couldn't sing (and still can't, nor hum on key on tune), I was still in the choir. Who does that? How did that happen? I'm still trying to figure that one out.

However, after becoming frustrated because I struggled to sing on key, I begged to quit the choir. However, "sitting on the bench" and doing nothing WAS NOT an option. But finally, I was granted permission to get out of the choir and my world of service opened as I joined the Usher Board. Not only did I serve there, but I also served in the nursery and in the secretary's office. While serving, there was A Lot of waiting for permission and not acting until you were "granted permission" to do things. This was control and in my adult life, I have learned not to be controlling. Walking the journey through counseling and Step Study/Celebrate Recovery has supported me along my journey.

Next came Saturday's church activities, which involved accompanying my mom and a group of ladies to serve residents in nursing homes and others in their own homes who were confined to the house due to an ailment. There were also other meetings, car washes, candy stripers meetings, cooking, selling desserts and dinners, as well as canvassing the community to minister to others and distribute spiritual tracks (literature). And then on Sunday, we'd repeat the schedule all over again.

Who can relate? If you can't relate, what was your experience with religion or with your chosen religious belief system?

During the summer, I attended Vacation Bible School. Not only did I attend Vacation Bible School at my church, but I also attended at two other community churches in my neighborhood where I lived. Even during all of this, somehow, I was still able to attend summer camp with the Girl Scouts.

My experience as part of the youth department was exciting, and there were always gatherings and activities taking place. We enjoyed church picnics and trips to Great America Amusement Park. We traveled on a huge conversion bus to visit other churches to recite Dr. King's speeches as part of being an Emmitt Till Player with Mother Mobley. We would also sing and attend musicals. This was during the time when there were choirs, and everyone wore robes, or black or blue bottoms, with the same color top.

What do you remember about events or activities at your place of worship?

If you haven't been a part of an organized religion, what do you remember about others who attend events and activities?

My world of speaking and oratory presentations was birthed at three points during my adolescent and young adult years.

First, while attending Sunday School, we were required to learn the golden text (a scripture) each week from the Sunday School lesson. At the end of each quarter, I stood in front of the church and recited each verse flawlessly. I recited Easter and Christmas speeches every year, and the older I got, the longer the speeches became. Also, at the end of vacation bible school, there was an oratory presentation.

The second point in time was as an Emmitt Till Player. This was a youth group who were responsible for learning and reciting Dr. King's speeches, to continue to share messages about civil rights and equality. We recited the speeches at my home church and traveled to other churches and organizations as well. Mother Mamie Till Mobley didn't play. You'd better study, prepare, and arrive on time. The expectation was to open your mouth, speak loudly, and pronounce each syllable and each word correctly. And standing tall was the only acceptable posture.

The third point in time my oratory speaking flourished was while reading our church announcements. Pastor Evangelist Arene Sample and Evangelist Dr. Ann Brickel were my spiritual mothers who loved me like a daughter. They groomed me and held high standards of perfection and efficiency. I can still hear, "We don't accept mediocre." They modeled how to stand tall while speaking and have clear articulation and pronunciation. They taught me how to study, how to prepare, how to teach and how to present. It is with them that I learned faith, wisdom, and how to be a leader. I learned how not to cause lasciviousness and how to be a virtuous woman. I was held to a high standard, (a very high standard as the two of them poured into me until their transition from Earth.

Perfection was my mindset and world view. Perfection is how I viewed myself, how I viewed others and what I expected from the world. This was not only as a result to my box of religion, but it was also true from my box of culture with the limiting belief that I had to "do more, be more and be better than" and my box of family with "You should, You Need To." After years and years of these deposits, I found myself counseling and attending a Step Study and Celebrate Recovery while focusing on recovering from perfection.

Remember there are always two sides to every coin, and this supports you with perspective. While on my self-discovery journey as I applied my CPR.ed framework, I embraced that there's a healthy side of perfectionism as well as an unhealthy side. Although the unhealthy side continues to pop up like popcorn from time to time, I have learned to silence that side of the coin as I manage the healthy side of perfectionism. I don't know who coined the phrase, but I stole it shamelessly, "done beats perfect." And that's what I do, instead of becoming stuck, paralyzed, not launching, nor moving forward, I get it done and keep it moving.

Who did you learn from?

I am fortunate to have a team! I am blessed to have a tribe!

Who is part of your team or tribe?

My mom, whom I love dearly, is the first to begin to lay a strong foundation for me. My godmother, Darlene Bailey, came alongside me as well, and both pushed me forward. I am also grateful to Sis. Loretta Haddox, Pastor Evangelist Arene Sample, Evangelist Cristine Johnson, Evangelist Dr. Ann Brickel, Prophetess Marilyn Brignac, Apostle Dr. Monique Fleming, and Pastor Katrina Farwig, who have poured abundantly into me along my journey. I even have a counselor, several coaches, and mentors, all of whom are females.

Their wisdom, knowledge, patience (oh it takes a lot of patience with me), unconditional love, guidance and teaching have been instrumental in my growth and building my foundation. There are others who are part of my team as well. Life is best navigated with the support of your team, village or community.

You see, my friend, I needed a team. And you need one, too!

Who are the people you trust that can be a part of your team, tribe, community to support you along your self-discovery journey?

Who will you ask to walk your journey with you to be your accountability partner?

Notice their gender, they are all women and in my box of religion "women are not expected to nor allow to hold certain titles or fill certain positions." As you can see, they did not allow limiting beliefs about roles, titles, the box of religion, nor historical and generational patterns, traditions, or expectations of others define who they are.

The same applies to you. You should not let any of those factors, limiting beliefs, your box of religion (or any other box) nor your belief system, define who you are.

My dear Pastor Madison Sample was also a part of my team, tribe and community. He always saw more in me than I saw in myself. He was incredibly patient and had an eye and gifting of drawing out much of who I am while showing me grace and mercy, and loving me unconditionally, like a daughter.

Who must you connect with that will see the best in you?

Remember, at the beginning of our discussion, we emphasized the importance of not walking your journey alone. You need the right support as you hit the reset button and step out of the boxes.

Take a moment to reflect on the outside of the box of religion, what awaits you?

Eat the Fish and Throw Away the Bone

As you continue to read, I encourage you to explore your religious experience from different perspectives. Also, I invite you to acknowledge that there are two sides of every coin as you gain an understanding, manage your emotions before you make decisions. You must make decisions about what you hold onto that's in service to you and what you let go of that's not in service to you.

Own your feelings as you reflect on your experience as it relates to your place of worship, organization, or faith. Be honest and real with yourself as you begin to stand face-to-face with reality. This will allow you to not only look at what wasn't right, what went wrong, or what may have hurt you or caused you pain, it's also important to acknowledge the positive things that took place, even if it's one thing (i.e., what you learned, friendships, etc.).

Yes, my spiritual foundation involved attending church, and participating in numerous rituals, patterns, and traditions, all while adhering to the expectations of others, adhering to legalism, even when some things didn't make sense. This perspective represents just one side of my experience. On the other side of the coin of my experiences, I learned valuable skills: leadership, study habits, preparation, organization, planning, speaking, and teaching skills. All these skills are fundamental and needed in my role as I teach, speak, and coach others.

I understand that while all these wonderful attributes were being developed in my life, I was simultaneously feeling suffocated by legalism within my box of religion. This aspect, admittedly, sucked life out of me, caused me to be drained and angry. Yes, it happened, and it's only several chapters of my story that have been written by others. And now, I am a proud author of my own life, I am thrilled to write the rest of my story and be in control of the narrative of my previous chapters that were written for me.

You can do the same. Relax, lean in, take your time, and just do it. Start crafting your own narrative, one that truly reflects who you are and who you want to be. Include in your story how you overcame the hurt and or challenges that existed in your religious box.

Restrictions: A Rough Road

There were so many countless restrictions I experienced growing up in church. I am crystal clear that I have become a rigid and stern person because of legalism. Many of the rituals, patterns, traditions, and expectations of others, imposed rules, by-laws, and expectations of the church did not align with biblical truth. This may also be true for some things from your church, place of worship, organization, or belief system. I have clarity and understanding that I had some good people in my life who gave me some bad doctrine. This bad doctrine was passed down from generation to generation, and they gave me only what they knew. It does not excuse the action, it just provides insight and allows me to heal knowing they were not intentional and vindictive in their actions.

During our church picnics, we had a good time. For the water activities, females weren't allowed to wear swimsuits. Instead, we wore shorts and a t-shirt, and males had to wear t-shirts with their swim trunks to get into the water.

In addition to women "not being allowed to," or "given permission to," hold certain positions and roles, we weren't allowed to speak from the pulpit. Instead, women had to speak from a small podium on the floor, off to the side in a corner. Women only "preached" on Women's Day and were typically known to teach Sunday School or a bible class. The place women were known to serve was as secretaries, administrators, church clerk, reading the announcements or providing water to the pastor, ministers or speaker for the day. As I reflect, I don't recall men serving in any of these capacities.

What roles did men and women fulfill at your place of worship? If you don't have a place of worship, what are your thoughts about this?

Talking about restrictions and limitations! The many restrictions and limitations were many and felt as if it equated to the number of grains in a 50-pound bag of rice. "You can't wear jewelry (except a wedding ring), you can't wear red lipstick, nor colored pantyhose. "Permission" was given to wear neutral colored pantyhose, nude, pecan, coffee, black, jet black or white. Even when wearing open-toe sandals, wearing a pair of pantyhose was still required.

I often wondered where these rules and restrictions originated.

What are your thoughts as to where these rules originated from?

Again, there were A LOT of rules and restrictions. For example, it was said that women should not resemble men, which was the rationale behind the rule that women were forbidden to wear pants. Naturally, my curiosity and inquisitive nature of asking questions often got me into trouble. But while asking questions, I was really trying to understand, especially considering that historically and culturally speaking, during certain eras, men wore dresses.

I recall when women at my church were "given permission" to wear pants, but only during the week and not on Sundays. So, I thought, "Okay, I'll take it." But it wasn't okay when I showed up at another church on a Saturday to attend a course to become licensed in ministry. It was the very first day, and I was chastised for wearing pants. This was at a place with the same religion, just a different church. I respect and honor the expectations of any church, organization, and place of worship. Just don't connect what people wear as a requirement for salvation.

At the beginning of the licensure class, we were told that everyone was to wear all white to the installation service. It wasn't until at the end of the course that it was stressed that the dress had to be "plain white with nothing on it". I already purchased my suit, and it was not plain. For me, and who I am, I like designs and things that sparkle. As I described my suit to the woman who was teaching, she asked me, "Can you take it back and purchase something plain?" The nerve of her to ask such a thing!

Talking about someone being furious and mad! I was hotter than 12 jalapeño peppers soaked in vinegar. And please don't ask me questions that you really don't want the answer to. My response was, "No, I can't." The look I got as the whole room stood still immediately made me feel like I said something wrong. But I was only answering the question. An older lady leaned over and whispered in my ear, "Sister Karen when in Rome, do as the Romans do." My reply was, "Maybe I don't need to be in Rome, nor here." Talking about a rollercoaster ride for me.

The weekend after the end of the course (yes, I did make it to the end) was the "big" installation day. Everyone was gathered in a room, waiting to enter the sanctuary, ready to march down the aisle and take our seats at the front of the church for the consecration service. Suddenly, there was a flurry of chatter and movement. I was trying to figure out what was happening when we were abruptly told to "take all earrings off."

Now wait a minute, what was going on? We had been told we could wear earrings if they were dime-sized and didn't dangle. Although mine met the requirements (they were cute and sparkling), I was once again silenced and muzzled as I asked questions to gain clarity and understand why. The stern and sharp look I received was all too familiar. There I was again, losing a part of myself again, as I was stuffed into a box that was entrenched in legalism. Talk about being suffocated in my box of religion! The fight to be me was rough and relentless.

What has your experience been with being restricted?

How do you recover when you are shut down?

If you have never been shut down, how did you navigate through life to not allow this to happen to you?

Another time I recall someone calling me after a service, asking, "Sister Karen, were you comfortable in the outfit you had on today?" My response was, "Yes, I was, were you comfortable with the outfit I had on today?" Well, that landed me locked in a room with this person for hours, being "rebuked" and "taught the right way" dressing modestly. I was then required to complete a study on the meaning of being modest and the meaning of anklets and why I shouldn't wear them. I was clear on the historical and cultural perspective of wearing anklets, and I wore them as a piece of jewelry to be adorned.

Although expectations and rules began to shift for some people and in some places of worship and organizations, they remained unchanged for others. So, do we, or don't we conform? Are we, or are we not supposed to follow the rules? And why? Why were some rules enforced and others not? None of this made sense to me. I can honor and respect expectations of religious facilities, or rules of "the house," as some may refer to the building where worship takes place. What I struggle with, is when expectations of the facilities or of a person, become the "law," that is connected to salvation and measures my spiritual health and well-being.

Whew, someone please hand me the reset button! I had to hit the reset button and step out of the box of religion.

What does it look like for you to hit the reset button and step out of your box of religion or identified belief system?

It is FREEING!

It was liberating as I decided to no longer be arrested or held hostage by the limiting messages. With this, it was thrilling to know that I can play games, games that had dice, and I can listen to music because all music is not "bad." And the beauty is, I'm not going to hell because I play games and listen to music.

Help me understand where did the expectation of not participating in these activities started and why?

Who knows?

Well, applying the CPR.ed process along my self-discovery journey, positioned me to manage through my feelings of having parts of my childhood stolen from me, after not being able to participate in school dances (i.e., homecoming, sock hops, etc.), nor participating in extracurricular classes at the park district or community centers. Instead of participating in tap, jazz, ballet, and modern dance classes, what was available to me were drama classes, arts and crafts, and sewing. How disappointing it was not to embrace "normal" childhood activities because of restrictions and legalism in the box of religion.

What's disappointing for you because of your box of religion, organization, or faith?

How did this shape who you are?

Because of the legalism inside my box of religion, I learned to be rigid, strict and inflexible. I learned to coerce and be manipulated and how to be coerced and manipulated. It was much easier at times to go along to get along. This led me to wear a mask and pretend, opposed to being truthful and authentic. What did this cost me? My innocence, peace and joy and as a result, I became angry because of who I had become, I was tired of watching the circus playing church and I left the church, but I never left my faith. Hear me, salvation is not about church, it's about relationships.

What decisions have you made to protect yourself, your peace and joy?

Religious Trauma: Scared to a Place of Fear

Although it's been over 35 years, I remember watching the movie "The Burning Hell" at church. For weeks, there was a lot of talk about a "movie night." And, of course, the youth were excited and looking forward to having a good time. After everyone arrived, the movie started, and I began to become unsettled.

The movie was about death and what happens to people who "don't live right." It portrayed a VERY gruesome vision of "what hell is like." The scenes were dark, with fire engulfing people who screamed, moaned, and groaned. It appeared unbearably hot, and there were worms or bugs crawling on people whose faces were distorted. It was HORRIBLE! I was SO confused – how did they know exactly what hell looks like while still alive? I wanted to ask how they knew, but I didn't dare.

After the movie, there was a LONG discussion about "if we didn't live right, we'd go to hell." Many things about this situation were just WRONG on many levels, starting with getting youth excited about watching "a movie."

Then, there was another "youth movie" and at that point, I absolutely did not want to go to church to watch called "Left Behind." This movie depicted the rapture, showing what it will appear when people who didn't make it into heaven after being left behind. The movie depicted scenes like cars crashing after drivers vanished while the world became a wreck and chaotic. One moment, a person would be in a conversation, and the next, they were gone.

Of course, you can guess what followed: another LONG talk after the movie, emphasizing the point that if we didn't "live right," we'd be left behind. I had many thoughts but no answers. And sadly, I was in an environment where asking questions was not welcomed. While riding home after the movie, and for a long time afterward, I was afraid to ride in cars, fearing the unpredictability of being in a car that crashes. For me, as a young adolescent, it was terrifying.

This made me furious, hurt, and angry. I became distrustful of adults in the church. This not only skewed my perception of people in the church, but it also made me distrustful to people in general, especially adults. I closed off, and I built a wall to protect myself. The walls protected me to keep people out, I later learned, unfortunately, it didn't allow me the opportunity to allow anyone to come in either. Over the years, I continued to become cold and resentful, as well as disinterested in the church and any related activities.

Remember we discussed that our experiences shape and impact who we become? My stance of being distrustful, cold and detached, impacted my relationships and how I connect and engage others. The fear bestowed upon me thrusts me to make emotional and bad decisions, instead of making wise decisions. After making bad decisions, I'd make another fear-based decision to fix the last one I made. Then, I'd make another fear-based wrong decision, trying to be perfect and "do the right thing," as prescribed by by-laws, legalism, historical and generational patterns, traditions and expectations of others. Talk about a circus! Talk about me running through my life unrestrained!

What "bad" decisions have you made, and then made another "bad" decision to fix the outcome of your first decision?

You may not have had the same experiences I had with religion, with your place of worship, organization, or your faith. Your experience is about you.

If you haven't had the same or a similar experience, what has been your experience?

What have you observed about how other people make decisions from a religious stance.

Listen, it's your time to run out of your religion box like a speeding bolt of lightning, to a place of re-setting, healing, to a place of freedom.

The Big Come Back

Despite the impact of my religious and religious trauma experience, I hit the reset button, and it changed my life. Others whom I have taught, spoken to and coached also hit the reset button; it changed their life. You, too, can hit the reset button and change your life. You are not responsible for what happened to you. Again, allow me the opportunity, I apologize for the experience you had. I invite you to take responsibility to heal, seek wise counsel, explore sound doctrine and engage in counseling or participate in a Step Study or Celebrate Recovery. As you do, take the pen and begin to write the next chapters in your life in a healthy fashion.

Take a moment to reflect on how to apply the emotional CPR.ed process as you step out of your religious box and again, begin to heal from historical and generational traditions, patterns and expectations of others. I encourage you to use this process to support you in processing your experiences. Please make the decision to no longer be choked, smothered, or have your life dictated by the box of religion. You know the drill: take the pen and begin to write the remaining chapters of your own story, as you shed the behaviors that's caused you to be dressed up and messed up.

Set yourself free from rituals, "church," legalism and historical patterns, traditions, and the expectations of others. As you do so, don't isolate yourself nor walk alone. Reach out to someone you trust to walk your journey with you. Get an accountability partner, a therapist, a coach, or connect with your religious leader and a trusted friend. Consult with a psychologist, a psychiatrist or a mental health specialist. This goes for your journey of getting out of the box of religion or any other box you identify.

Be yourself — who you truly are. Live life and experience freedom. I deeply appreciate living from a place of freedom.

What does freedom look like for you?

For me, freedom means stopping cycles and getting out of the box. Getting out of the box to a growth mindset and being mindful of the legacy I leave for the next generation. This involves working through my emotions related to my religious experiences.

I needed to heal from the unfortunate incident in that communion was canceled until further notice due to a disagreement over the length of and shade of white for the dresses women wore to serve communion. There was also a debate and misunderstanding regarding the shade of while the shoes had to be and the height of their heels.

I needed to manage through the anger and disappointment as I shuddered while reflecting on a time when a young girl was barred from participating in youth activities because she couldn't attend practice every Saturday. She couldn't attend because she spent time with her dad every other weekend. On the other weekends, her mother and grandmother would take her to practice and work with her during the week to ensure she was prepared. This situation baffled me, raising questions about what happens when you have a family that doesn't fit the mold of a "traditional" family, consisting of one mom and one dad having children and they all reside in the same home. And what exactly defines "a traditional family"?

I had to work through the impact of my emotions because of these situations, and you need to work through your emotions as well because of your experiences. If none of what I've shared applies to you, please be patient and non-judgmental as other people journey to crawl out of the box.

As I maneuvered along my self-discovery journey and applied the emotional CPR.ed process, I had to embrace the reality that my birth family of origin is blended and that my current nuclear family is blended. I had to not be in denial that I carried church hurt after being shamed and reprimanded following becoming divorced while parenting an infant child. But my new freedom, outside of the box, allows me to release the guilt and shame that my family is not "traditional" as the "church" expected and upheld "traditional families." Being a single parent and the head of my household following a divorce, I am a person who is creative, resourceful, strong, has time management and good problem-solving skills. Moving away from legalism and from the "should's and suppose to's" help me to discover truth and connect with myself.

I know, emotions suck! And unaddressed emotions are even worse and will take the wind right out of you like a sailboat in a storm. Owning, embracing, and managing my emotions afforded me the opportunity to think clearly and make sound and wise decisions for myself in my life. I decided that I would no longer be held hostage by rituals, legalism, expectations of others, or religion. I decided that I was no longer willing to tolerate foolishness from any box that was in my life. There's no perfect church, nor perfect place of worship, or organization because they all are made up of imperfect people like me and like you, like us all.

How many of you are perfect?

As you work on becoming your true self again, remember to explore things from all perspectives, to look at both sides of the coin, and to forgive. Keep in mind that there have been, and currently are, good people in your life. Sometimes, these good people may have given you some incorrect or bad doctrine or information that didn't align with biblical truth simply because that's all they knew.

I don't mention this to dismiss what's happened nor to dismiss your experience. I mention it because it's an important reality to consider, swallow and accept. They likely just passed down what they knew from generation to generation. I suggest that you try to separate the person from behaviors and their flaws.

Take a moment to reflect on the positive contributions these people have made.

Let's drill deeper and look at this from a different perspective.

You are a good person, right?

I too see myself as a good person. And, despite our best intentions, we, too, sometimes give advice or provide information that isn't entirely wise and sound. This is why there's a need for you to connect with yourself and know for yourself what you believe and don't believe. With this understanding, you can then share information and knowledge that strengthens, uplifts, encourages, and fosters growth for the next generation, and generations to follow.

Decide to leave a legacy that allows people to be who they are. The pendulum swings both ways. Just as you want people to forgive and have grace towards you, you must do the same for others.

Decide to thrive as you release people and release yourself from the residue of your experiences. When you do, this then allows you to be free, to be yourself.

Decide to heal, seek truth and sound doctrine for yourself.

Hit the reset button as you walk in transparency, authenticity, and stand in your truth. Stay focused because you are headed to freedom.

What do you believe?

Why do you believe what you believe?

I teach my children and encourage others to know for themselves what they believe (or don't believe) and why they believe it (or don't believe it). I encourage you to do the same. Be who you are and not what rituals, legalism, religion, and historical and generational patterns, traditions, and expectations of others have told you to be.

Pause for a moment and take a deep breath. This is the last of the four boxes we will discuss. You are officially bound freedom, and it's time for you to get out of the box.

No more compliance! No more pretending!

Hurry, go to the next chapter, Identity ReSet 6: Freedom Bound: Get Out of Your Box! It's your turn to live a life of freedom in all areas of your life.

Identity ReSet 6:
Freedom Bound:
GET OUT OF YOUR BOX!

Freedom Bound: Get Out of Your Box!

It's Your Turn

Race Box

Wow! What a journey!

I am proud of my race, culture, and heritage! All races have their share of success and challenges. You are not defined by your race. There may be limiting messages, or superior messages, within your race, but they don't have to become your truth or your reality. You don't have to succumb to historical and generational traditions, patterns and expectations of others.

What's your truth? Get out of the box!

Family Box:

I love my family! I am SO grateful for my family. No family is "perfect," and all families have challenges. Forgive people, love them, and don't pass flawed information from generation to generation as you get out of the boxes. Make decisions that align with your values. It's okay that you make decisions different from those of your family.

What's your truth? Get out of the Box!

Roles Box:

I am me! Yes, with roles, there are "said expectations" that "males should or shouldn't" and "females should or shouldn't." Who created this? How did we get here? These expectations don't define you. Despite roles or titles, you carry, you don't have to live up to the myths of the title, nor expectations of others.

What's your truth? Get out of the box!

Religion Box:

Again, I wouldn't trade my spiritual foundation for anything. There is no "perfect" religion, place of worship, or person within your religion or place of worship. Despite titles and positions, or the length of time someone has been part of their religion, EVERYONE has flaws and faces challenges, EVERYONE. Always remember, there's a significant difference between religion and personal relationship. Every religion has its successes and challenges.

You have had, or currently have, some genuinely good people in your life who, unfortunately, may have passed down incorrect information or flawed knowledge. Forgive them and continue to love them. It's your responsibility to position yourself to obtain correct misinformation or sound doctrine as you discover the truth for yourself. It's never too late to make course correct to support you to leave a legacy for the next generation.

What's your truth? Get out of the box!

Pathway to You:

1. Forgive! Forgive yourself! Forgive others! Forgive, and set yourself free!
2. Be kind, gentle, and patient with yourself along your self-discovery journey. As a result of your experiences, you may have had ups and

downs and need to manage through hurt, anger, frustration, or other emotions. Don't stay there; your experiences do not define you.

3. Hit the reset button and apply the emotional CPR.ed process. You will gain clarity about how you have been shaped. You will come to understand what and how things happened in your life (purpose it served). In doing so, it's important for you to pause, take a deep breath, and embrace reality through the process. No more being in denial, packing, or ignoring your thoughts and feelings. When we do, it causes health concerns, stress and mental health concerns.

4. Courageously ride the waves and embrace each of your emotions as normal. Your emotions are messages to you. Listen to the messages; they are a gift to you. Managing your emotions allows you to think clearly and make sound and wise decisions as you respond, as opposed to reacting. Commit to yourself that you will no longer make emotional decisions based on your boxes that breed historical and generational patterns, traditions, and expectations of others. Commit to being truthful about behaviors and expectations that no longer serve you along your self-discovery journey. Live YOUR life, thrive and experience freedom.

5. I invite you to look at both sides of the coin. Explore your experience and situations from different perspectives. Looking at both sides allows you to live a balanced life. As you view experiences and situations from both sides of the coin and from different perspectives, pause, reflect, and take a moment for yourself. If you don't, you will only look at the dark side of how things shaped you to become who you are. Be okay to look beneath the surface.

   What box do you need to look at from both perspectives?

   In doing so, how will this shift you to a place of being truthful, honest and authentic?

My experience of looking at both sides of the coin has helped me embrace who I am. I've noticed others who I teach, speak to, and coach have the same experience. You, too, can have the same freeing experience; join me.

6. Remember, there are chapters of your life that were written for you. And now, my friend, you get to take the pen and write your next chapters. YOU get to be the author of your story. What an opportunity! You no longer must live in any boxes. Keep in mind, the limiting messages will continue to pop up in your life at any given moment, like popcorn. You must learn how to arrest your thoughts as you stand in and speak your truth. Again, the limiting messages do not define you, despite the trauma, generational trauma, secondary traumatic stress, etc, you have experienced. Give those messages back to whoever gave them to you. You have the responsibility to heal, and you get to dictate how you live your life.

   What decisions do you need to make for yourself?

   It's your turn now!

   Where would you like to start?

7. Identify the boxes that are present in your life.

   If you don't relate to the box of race, family, roles, or religion, what other boxes exist for you?

   Whatever your boxes are, get out of them! If it's a box of how you manage or don't manage money, a box of superiority, inferiority, or poverty, get out of the box. If your box is the box of hurt, guilt, shame, depression, or a box of mental health impairment, disability, or illness, get out of the box! Maybe it's a dependency box or a co-dependent box; get out! Whatever the box, you name it and get out of it! Looking in those boxes will thrust you into a journey of self-discovery. I shared my awakening experience, which is transforming.

   What does your awakening moment look like?

What to Expect on your Self-Discovery Journey

Expect that everyone will not embrace your journey nor support you while getting out of the boxes. Learn how to set and honor boundaries you set. Learn the art of allowing people to feel how they feel and say what they want to say. That's their business, and you don't have to take on their beliefs, thoughts, feelings, opinions and emotions as your own.

Gain clarity about the reasons behind the historical and generational patterns, traditions, and expectations of others. Expect some people to be stuck, unwilling to change or don't know how to change embrace your change. Some people are comfortable with what has been passed down from generation to generation, and that's okay. Some of what they believe may be their truth, but not necessarily the actual truth or fact. You get to choose what no longer serves you.

Prepare to be liberated. As you run out of your boxes, be intentional not to allow anyone nor anything suck you back in. Expect to protect your mindset and emotions as you establish boundaries. It may feel weird or uncomfortable at first, but it's important to stay committed to it.

You may have experienced being controlled or manipulated, in efforts to get you to comply with many said expectations. Remember, people may have lived their lives and complied with ignorance, fear, or a need for acceptance. You get to manage things differently in your life.

Give yourself permission to process and think for yourself as you shift and pivot when necessary. Expect that some people will support and accept you as you discover who you are and live your life, while others may not. Remember, this is okay, and the historical and generational traditions, patterns, and expectations of others do not dictate decisions for your life.

What's your goal? To step out of your box, to be yourself, be honest, transparent and authentic as you live your life. Aim to live a thriving life, a life of freedom.

Yes, fear may be present with you, take one step at a time as you hit the reset.

Take a Step

Be bold and courageous as you explore your boxes and then stand in truth as if you are authentic. It may require you to move against the grain, operate outside of the norm, or stand-alone. I've been there, and in the process, my emotions felt like I was riding a roller coaster with 10-foot drops and 180 or 360-degree turns, all while being jolted abruptly. At other times, it felt as if I was on the ride, "The Floor Drop," as the ride spun and spun, and the floor torpedoed from under my feet. But I had to pause and decide to no longer live life going in circles.

Yes, at times, you will feel a lot of emotions and feel like you are a mess, like the mass destruction following the aftermath of an 8-mile-wide hurricane or tornado ripping through town at 225 miles an hour with no sight in mind. And if you think that's a challenge, imagine what will happen and how you will feel if remain in denial, people-please, and live up to other people's expectations for YOUR life. Take the pen and write your own story. You will experience FREEDOM!

Roll with it as I did during my awakening moment you read about in chapter one. Yes, you may feel like a mess, like mass destruction following the aftermath of a 40-mile-wide hurricane or tornado ripping through town at 225 miles per hour, with no end in sight. The beauty of weathering the storm is that you get to dig amongst the rubble to finally rediscover yourself, how exciting.

You get to live YOUR life. You get to just be YOU!

Yes, it can be alarming and VERY uncomfortable to shift and transition. This is because what you have learned, thought, felt, and known your entire, something is missing. As you journey, it might feel as if things are crashing down as you discover that some things are not true or do not align with your reality or your values.

It is indeed uncomfortable to step out of your comfort zone as you learn, unlearn, and relearn. At the same time, it is even more uncomfortable not to be in good emotional, mental, and physical health as you attempt to live up to someone else's expectations or live as someone you are not. But the outcome of being yourself and experiencing freedom is worth persevering through your journey.

Stay with the process!

Don't remain stuck like a spider on its web. Step off the never-ending roller coaster or merry-go-round that has left you with a fixed mindset, merely struggling to keep up and survive. Embrace a growth mindset as you learn new things and discover who you are.

Hit the reset button!

Transition well!

Thrive in your life and experience freedom!

After your awakening experience, climb out of the box and embrace your freedom. Use your voice to speak from your heart, standing in your truth and being authentic. It's time to unpack years of baggage and unravel miles of confusion in your life. Take that step, hit the reset button, restructure, and restart how you live.

No more patterns! No more doing it for others!

Take one last look on the next page, as you take a deep breath and prepare to develop your next step and read, One Last Message: What's Next? YOU!

the outcome of being yourself and experiencing freedom is worth the strength through your journey.

Stay with the process.

Don't remain stuck in the mundane cycle with the same old tired, boring, rote routines. [illegible] You with a fixed mindset lacks imagination to keep up and succeed. Embrace a growth mindset as you learn new things and discover who you are.

Hit the reset button.

Transform yourself.

To transform your life and experience freedom:

Let your awesome, extraordinary brilliance out of the box and embrace your freedom. Use your voice to speak from your heart, standing in your truth and being authentic. It's time to unpack years of baggage and strip all layers of conditioning in your life. Take action, hit the reset button, transform, and restart how you live.

No more patterns! No more doing it [illegible]!

Take one last look at the old you. Take a deep breath and prepare to develop your new self and vibe. One Last Release. What's NEW YOU.

One Last Message:
What's Next:

HIT THE RESET BUTTON!

What's Next? YOU!

Go Forth

Who are you?

What do you need to say no to?

While saying no, what are you saying yes to?

What do you REALLY believe?

You are the captain of your life!

Put yourself first as you say yes to yourself. Get in tune with what you must say no to. YOU MATTER!

Reflect on where you are. Be gut-wrenchingly honest with yourself and stop living in denial. Make decisions based on reality, not what you want it to be, "what it should be", or "what it could be." Deal with those thoughts, feelings, and emotions you don't share with anyone or only speak to them in your mind.

Identify and connect with how your box of race, family, roles, religion, or your self-identified box has shaped who you have become. Be authentic and honest with yourself as you explore the question, "Who Am I."

As you do so, stand in your truth! Not the truth of your historical and traditional generational patterns, traditions, and expectations of others. You get to decide what you keep and what you discard from what has been passed to you from prior generations. Then, be mindful of what you pass to the next generation as you leave a legacy.

To support you along your journey, apply emotional CPR.ed process, as you discover YOU. Get ready to gain Clarity, understand Purpose, and stand face-to-face with Reality.

While doing so, give yourself permission to own, feel, and embrace each emotion (emotions are normal) you experience.

You MUST manage your emotions (emotions are normal) to support you in making sound **Decisions** along your discovery journey. Don't make decisions based on your thinking and feeling cycle that led to unwelcome behaviors, nor the thinking, feeling cycle of others that lead to unwelcome behaviors. You get to decide how you navigate your boxes, what YOU want, and journey according to what YOU believe. As you continue to discover who you are, choose to stretch yourself and stay away from your familiar fixed mindset. Have an open and growth mindset as you view your boxes and situations from different perspectives and both sides of the coin.

Get ready to live YOUR life of joy as you thrive and walk in freedom.

Now, let's celebrate your commitment as you move upward, forward, and onward. Kudos to you for deciding not to live another day inside of a box as you decide not to live another year the same.

As you discover who you are, let's celebrate as you become liberated from fear and rid yourself of being frozen with the "what ifs." You are courageous! It's time to use your voice as you be yourself.

What does freedom look like for you?

What does thriving look like for you?

What legacy will you leave for the next generation?

Give yourself a hand, give yourself a hug, and celebrate for taking the first step to being yourself. How exciting!

One, two, three, GO!

Welcome to a life of freedom! Welcome to a life of thriving!

It's ALL about YOU!

Yes, To Awakening! Yes, To Transformation!

Now that you have the language and tools to support you as you transition well, be yourself, and live YOUR life. I would love to hear about your experience. Contact me at info@kdtglobalconsulting.com or you can visit www.kdtglobalconsulting.com to share your experience.

#nomorefear

#nomoreboxes

#nomorepeoplepleasing

#develop

#evolve

#grow

#freedom

#thrive

#growthmindset

Acknowledgments

Through the years, there are many of you who have impacted my life in different ways. It's impossible to note everyone, and there is not enough space here to acknowledge each of you. Please know that I greatly appreciate you all

To my village, my family; thank you to my awesome husband Patrick, I love you. What a privilege and honor to have a blended family and thank my stunning children, Faythe, Kaleb, Torianna, Patrick II, Gabriel and Javell, I love you. Thank you to my amazing parents, Jack Sr. and Lessie, and to my fabulous siblings, Ella, Jack Jr., Michael and Laronda, I love. Thank you to all my paternal and maternal family. I love you all.

To my friends who have helped keep me together, Marla Matthews, Marsheila Harris, Veronica Boyd, Tonisha Swanson Allison, Debra Lozano, Theresa Hayes, and all the others who are not listed. Your love and support are greatly appreciated. I love you.

To my tribe, thank you to Pastors Madison and Arene Sample, Evangelist Dr. Ann Brickel, Sis. Loretta Haddox, Evangelist Christine Johnson, Prophetess Marilyn Brignac, Apostle Dr. Monique Fleming, Pastor Katrina Farwig and my Godmother, Darlene Bailey for your love and pouring into me. I appreciate each of you and I love you all.

To my professional tribe who have poured into me and supported me to be my best, Ruth Martin, Monico Eskridge, Matthew Gyger and Judy Tudor, I have watched you and learned as you modeled how to be a great leader. I appreciate you and thank you.

To my counselor, Madison Flores, Bethany Kammert, who helped me along the way as I walked through my own self-discovery journey. You supported me as I unpacked my backpack and luggage and as I worked to get out of my boxes. You allowed me to speak freely and honestly, with no judgement as I acknowledged and spoke of things I never shared with anyone. You held a safe space for me, as I navigated through standing face to face with reality, with unprocessed emotions and trauma while using the EMDR approach.

To my support, Keith Stark, Ron Eckman, Stefanie Nieto-Johnson, Michelle Maloy Dillon, Tina Meyers (who facilitated my life changing 15-minute volunteer experience), Life on Fire, Life Surge, and Ignite Life. Your expertise, guidance and support have helped to thrust me forward.

To John Baker and Rick Warren, between participating in Step Study, Celebrate Recovery, and reading/working through "Life's Healing Choices," my life was not turned upside down, and instead, my WHOLE life was turned right side up, thank you.

To my sheros and heroes who kept me sane and focused during many challenging and turbulent times. Your life, your messages and/or songs have impacted me; Priscilla Schriver, Joyce Meyers, Steven Furtick, Nick Vujicic, Maverick City, Juanita Bynum, Donald Lawrence, Pastor Matthew Stevenson, William McDowell, Elevation Worship, Hillsong United, Bethel Music, Donnie McClurkin, Oprah Winfrey, Kirk Franklin, Sonnie Badu, Michael Jackson (Man In The Mirror), Bruno Mars (Just the Way You Are), Rihanna (Diamonds), and Destiny's Child (Survivor). To each of you, thank you!

About the Author

Karen D. Tyler, M.S.W., CPCC
Coach, Author, Speaker

Karen has walked her own journey of self-discovery, as she hit the reset button, to get out of her boxes to just be herself. In search of exploring the question, "Who Am I, she experienced EMDR through counseling, participated in Step Study, as well as large and small groups with Celebrate Recovery. This helped her to better understand the impact of historical and generational traditions, patterns and expectations of others. Karen coined the CPR.ed strategy, and this supported her to look at things from different perspectives to support with her decision making.

Karen spends her time with her awesome husband, Patrick, blended family of 6 children, 2 grandchildren, and with her parents, siblings, nieces, nephews, Godchildren and extended family and friends. She also enjoys desserts, skating, watching movies, and traveling.

Karen serves as a speaker, Certified Co-active Professional Life Coach, author, mentor, and serves on several Leadership Teams. She earned her Bachelor and Master of Social Work degree from Jane Addams College of Social Work at University of Illinois at Chicago.

Not only has lived experience, but also for nearly 30 years, she has served hospitals, private, public, and religious organizations; as well as within the child welfare, social and human service arenas, and workforce/organization development. Karen enjoys teaching at colleges, while challenging minds of students, and emerging leaders within Bachelor's and master's Programs of Social Work.

Karen Tyler is a best-selling author, author of "Identity Reset," and contributing author of "Let the Daughters Arise."

Karen is a torch that ignites possibilities, while empowering and mobilizing others. She is a catalyst for transformation, growth and development. Karen is a pioneer and a visionary, who honors excellence, and is described as passionate, kind, and hardworking.

Karen is the Founder and CEO of Reset Rethink Solutions LLC., and KDT Global Consulting.

Reset Rethink Solutions provides organization development, sustainability planning, implementation science, leadership and professional development support (info@reset-rethink.com, www.reset-rethink.com).

KDT Global Consulting provides support with personal and family development, conflict resolution, blended families with a focus on life and legacy planning to build future generations (info@kdtglobalconsulting.com, www.kdtglobalconsulting.com).

www.ingramcontent.com/pod-product-compliance
Lightning Source LLC
LaVergne TN
LVHW051245080426
835513LV00016B/1754

* 9 7 9 8 9 8 9 0 6 3 0 0 0 *